WHALE SHARKS

WHALE

SHARKS

THE GIANTS
OF NINGALOO REEF

GEOFF TAYLOR

FOREWORD BY
EUGENIE CLARK

Angus&Robertson
An imprint of HarperCollins*Publishers*

To my father
Eric Frank Taylor
1919–1990

Two roads diverged in a wood, and I —
I took the one less traveled by,
And that has made all the difference.

Robert Frost, 'The Road Not Taken', 1916

An Angus & Robertson Publication

Angus&Robertson, an imprint of
HarperCollins*Publishers*
25 Ryde Road, Pymble, Sydney NSW 2073, Australia
31 View Road, Glenfield, Auckland 10, New Zealand
77–85 Fulham Palace Road, London W6 8JB, United Kingdom
10 East 53rd Street, New York NY 10022, USA

First published in Australia in 1994

Copyright © Geoff Taylor 1994

National Library of Australia
Cataloguing-in-Publication data:

Taylor, Geoff (John Geoffrey), 1950– .
  Whale sharks.

  Bibliography.
  Includes index.
  ISBN 0 207 18498 4.

  1. Whale shark. 2. Ningaloo Marine Park (W.A.). I. Title.

597.31

Cover photography by Geoff Taylor
Cover designed by Darian Causby
Book design by Kerry Klinner
Illustrations by Russell Jeffery
Printed in Australia by Griffin Press

9 8 7 6 5 4 3 2 1
97 96 95 94

FOREWORD

Whale sharks have long been considered one of the rarest and most wonderful of sea monsters. Every sighting of a whale shark creates a sensation, even amongst the most experienced anglers, scuba divers and oceanographers. It is certainly the dream of every avid diver to be able to swim with one — I had been diving for 34 years before that dream came true for me.

Although whale sharks were long known to range the tropical seas around the world, shark specialists considered appearances of whale sharks unpredictable. A dozen years ago, Geoff Taylor, a medical doctor at the hospital in Exmouth, Western Australia, started taking his family diving off Ningaloo Reef. He was so taken by his first encounter with a whale shark that since then, he has devoted all his spare time to searching the sea for them. He was the first person to keep detailed records of individual whale sharks. And he began to see a pattern, an unusual abundance of sharks coming in to feed off Ningaloo Reef in late March and April. He could predict to within a few days when they would appear, and correlated this with the plankton bloom that followed the massive annual spawning of corals on Ningaloo Reef — a phenomenon being studied by marine biologist Chris Simpson.

Even though whale sharks are the largest fish in the sea and feed near the surface, they are rarely seen unless you are very close to them. Geoff made a plan to methodically scan the waters off Ningaloo Reef using both boats and aeroplanes. He was able to record over 150 sightings of whale sharks in the span of a few weeks and opened up a field of research for scientists — and a field day for divers wanting to fulfil their dreams of swimming with whale sharks.

It is a great pleasure for me to write the Foreword to Geoff's book, which tells the story of his amazing breakthrough in understanding the whale sharks. Thanks to his efforts over the past 12 years, we can now predict the appearance of whale sharks off Ningaloo Reef. This may further our understanding of other locations where whale sharks gather.

Geoff's studies should be supported and encouraged, for he is the only person in the world who is focusing his trained eye and expert abilities on the study of this most magnificent fish. He is on location at Ningaloo every year, with the energy and means to gather data, trying every method — even satellite-tracking — to understand when and why the sharks come in such large numbers to the reef. Geoff continues to fill in the missing pieces about the little-known biology and habits of one of the greatest creatures that has ever lived on our planet.

It is a lucky coincidence that Geoff, with his curiosity and love for the sea, happened to take up medical practice near the exceptionally rich waters of Ningaloo Reef, and discovered the conditions that lead to the gathering of whale sharks, and the other giant plankton feeders of the oceans — the baleen whales and manta rays. I have never dived in such an abundance of marine life. Geoff advised David Doubilet and me on the best time to visit Ningaloo to do an article for *National Geographic* on whale sharks. We are grateful to Geoff for this highlight in our lives.

Ningaloo Reef is a unique place in the vast oceans of the world. Wisely, the Australian government has recognised this and declared it a National Park, offering protection to this precious resource. Let us pray that this area adjacent to the Indian Ocean, nourished by nutrient-laden upwellings and the complex movements of the Leeuwin Current, will continue to reveal and to help solve some of the most intriguing and important mysteries of the sea.

Dr Eugenie Clark
Senior Research Scientist, University of Maryland
March 1994

CONTENTS

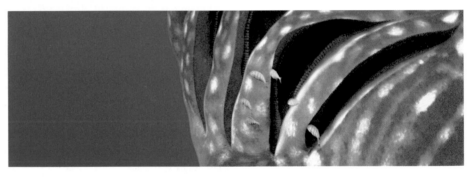

ACKNOWLEDGMENTS

Over the years, many friends and family members have assisted me with many different aspects of the whale shark project — in the early days with the filming, and more latterly with the research.

I would like to thank the following organisations and people: the Australian National Parks and Wildlife Service for their assistance and the provision of funding in 1990 and 1991; the staff of the Western Australian Department of Conservation and Land Management for their assistance, co-operation and advice; the Western Australian Fisheries Department for their co-operation; Frances Berrigan and Cicada Films for assistance in 1992; Professor Gordon Grigg for several years of support and advice; Dr Helene Marsh for much-needed advice regarding aerial surveys; Peter Arscot and the pilots of Exmouth Air Charters for all the aerial work; David Doubilet, Rodney Fox and George King for inviting me to accompany them in 1991; David Heaphy for his assistance on *Business II* in 1992 to 1994; Peter Hall, of Diving Ventures, for sponsoring ongoing research; divemaster Rae Prokojes for his assistance with data; the aerial observers — the late Jim Wolfenden, John Blinkhorn, Les Eadon, Pat Willis, Lucy Huckle, Chris Norris, Pat Bellar and Ric Karniewicz; Peter Harding for his observations of coral spawning at Coral Bay; Bruce Mate and Sharon Nieukirk of Oregon State University for their assistance with satellite-tracking; particular thanks to Eugenie Clark for her support, and for writing the Foreword to this book; and my wife, Joanna, for all her help and patience.

On various boats over the years, I have been ably assisted by Peter Moore, Adrian Mitchell, Allan Sutton, Bill Winchester, Ian Turner, Henning Nielsen, Les Eadon, Chris Willis, Duke Huckle and Andrew Linford.

Thanks also to David Moore, David and Elizabeth Parer, Tony Bomford, Dennis Robinson, Chris Hooke, Adrian Kuballa, Mark Hantler and Ed Jowett.

Finally, I would also like to thank the following people for assistance in the identification of species and advice on biological matters: Dr Gerry Allan and Diana Jones, Museum of Western Australia; David Ritz, University of Tasmania; Dr Jack Greenwood, University of Queensland; and Dr Susan Osborne, of the Department of Conservation and Land Management, Exmouth. Also, thanks to Dr John Stevens, CSIRO, Hobart, for reading the manuscript.

INTRODUCTION

The whale shark is one of the largest creatures on this planet and the largest fish in the world. It has intrigued naturalists for many years. Despite its size, it is so rarely seen that until recently, very little was known about it. There was nowhere in the world where whale sharks could be found predictably, so no one had attempted to study the species. This situation changed when it was discovered that at certain times of the year, large numbers of whale sharks gathered at Ningaloo Reef, off the isolated north-west coast of Western Australia.

I have tried in this book to give an overview of the little that is known about the whale shark, and also to tell my personal story, of how a chance encounter at Ningaloo Reef with one of the species led to a quest to again find these rare

creatures and to film them. From this beginning, my interest broadened, and I began to undertake a much deeper study of the whole ecology of the sharks and of the coral reef at Ningaloo.

My formal biological training is entirely medical, but I have always had a passionate interest in wildlife, and an ambition to be a wildlife photographer. I have also always wanted to study the ecology of a complete ecosystem.

These interests took me in two quite different directions. On the one hand, I hoped to be involved as a photographer in making a documentary about the reef and the sharks. On the other, I became increasingly involved in researching the sharks and trying to find out why they appear in such numbers at Ningaloo Reef. Ultimately, I failed in my first ambition, as I ended up in front of the camera rather than behind it. However, the research continues.

This book begins with a description of the adventures of diving with the whale sharks. Chapters about the biology and the history of the sharks follow. The geography and natural history of the North–West Cape region of Australia are discussed in Chapter 4, where I provide an overview of the reef and the food chain that revolves around it. This is largely my own interpretation based upon personal observations, and is, at times, speculative — there is still a great deal that is not fully understood about tropical ecosystems. In Chapters 5 to 7, I give a more personal account of my involvement with the sharks, including the media race to

film the sharks and the research that I have undertaken. The book concludes with a discussion of the conservation issues that relate to both the whale shark — whose status appears to be 'vulnerable' — and Ningaloo Reef, which is very much under threat.

Throughout my quest for the sharks, many friends have given their support and assistance; none more so than my wife, Joanna. I used to joke that she had promised to follow me to the ends of the earth, and that I had taken her there. Perth, in Western Australia, is said to be the remotest city on earth, and the town of Exmouth is 1250 km (750 miles) north of Perth. While Exmouth may be very remote, it is also the site of the United States Naval Communications Base, and in the time that I lived there, during the 1980s and early 1990s, it had a unique, cosmopolitan community. It proved to be a fantastic place to raise children — a safe environment, isolated from the problems of the modern world — and I wish to pay tribute to the people of Exmouth who made it such a special community.

It is my greatest regret that my father did not live to see this book published, succumbing to cancer in 1990. He had found it difficult to understand why I ensconced myself in a remote part of Australia, away from my family in England, to pursue an elusive shark. Perhaps this book would have provided him with an explanation.

There are parts of this book that will be considered controversial in some quarters, particularly the statements on environmental issues concerning Ningaloo Reef. There is a great need for a pro-active stance to be taken so that this environment will be understood and protected. My research efforts have merely scratched the surface of what is occurring at Ningaloo. A tremendous opportunity exists for further research into such areas as coral reefs, tropical food chains, nitrogen fixation and of course the whale shark, subjects that are way beyond the resources of an individual.

If this book succeeds in stimulating further discussion and research, and a greater appreciation of the unique environment of Ningaloo Reef and its gentle and elusive visitor, the whale shark, particularly on the part of government, then it will have succeeded.

CHAPTER 1

DIVING WITH THE WHALE SHARK

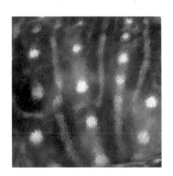

We had been searching Ningaloo Reef for several hours with little success. The wind had dropped and the temperature was rising towards 38°C (100°F). We decided to stop the boat and have a snorkel close to the reef, just to cool off. Three of us were in the water when suddenly there was an excited shout from the boat: 'Shark! Shark!'

THE LURE OF
WILD AND RARE CREATURES

For anyone interested in wildlife, one of the most exciting experiences is to sight a rare species; even more so if the creature can be examined at close quarters. For a diver there are few experiences that can compare with that of diving with whales, dolphins, manta rays, huge cod or sharks. Underwater, there is always an element of danger, but the ultimate 'buzz' is to have contact with a wild creature. The larger the creature, the greater the excitement.

The whale shark is one such creature. For many years it was considered rare and elusive. Only a few divers had been fortunate enough to have a chance encounter with this huge animal. And because of its enormous proportions, its inquisitiveness, and its gentle nature, all were enthralled by the experience.

One of the few surviving giants of the ocean, the whale shark has remained a mystery to anglers, divers and scientists alike until very recently. However, the discovery that whale sharks appear each year at Ningaloo Reef off the North-West Cape, a remote area of the Western Australian coast, changed that. Studies of the sharks at Ningaloo Reef over a ten-year period showed that their annual appearance was in fact predictable. This resulted in divers from all over the world flocking to Exmouth, a small town at the northern end of the North-West Cape peninsula, in search of one of the ultimate diving adventures. It also presented people such as myself, who wanted to learn more about the whale sharks, with the opportunity to study this fascinating creature in the wild.

In the vanguard of the diving adventurers were the photographers. Photojournalists and wildlife photographers poured into Exmouth in the early 1990s in a race against time and each other to get the best photo, the closest close-up, the most original angle for the magazines of the world. Film and television companies from Japan, New Zealand, the United Kingdom, the United States and Italy, as well as some local Australian companies, also entered the race to get footage of this rare creature.

BELOW: *Norwegian Bay, with Point Cloates in the distance, is in the heart of Ningaloo Reef. The line of surf marks the place where the reef divides the shallow lagoon from the deep waters of the Indian Ocean. An old whaling station, which has long since fallen into disuse, is situated in the middle of Norwegian Bay.*

THE FIRST UNDERWATER ENCOUNTER

For every diver, the first underwater encounter with a creature as impressive as the whale shark is a very personal and memorable experience. My first encounter, in 1983, took three years of dreaming, planning and waiting to achieve. I had become determined to find the sharks, to dive with them and to film them underwater with my Super-8 cinecamera. In 1982, I moved with my family to Exmouth to work as a doctor, thus bringing the possibility closer. The very first trip I made on the water there — a fishing trip in May 1982 — I sighted two whale sharks. Throughout the rest of that year, I made numerous searches, without success. It wasn't until March 1983 that I finally located another whale shark.

It was one of those glorious days on Ningaloo Reef: the weather was good, without the usual March sea-breeze, so the sea was calm. The Indian Ocean swells were rolling in and pounding onto the reef as Peter Moore and I motored along the reef front with trolling lines astern. There was little action

BELOW: *Diving down to inspect a whale shark. This Japanese snorkeller was so excited at the prospect of diving with a jimbe (the Japanese word for whale shark), he didn't finish putting on his wetsuit.*

from the game fish that morning, so after two hours we stopped and tried some bottom-fishing, but the swells were more than my stomach could take and it was not long before we were moving again.

Suddenly, there it was, the creature for which I had spent almost a year searching. It appeared as a huge shape, coming up to the surface right under the bow of the boat. I was overcome with excitement as I stood up on the seat, clutching the windscreen, and looked down at one of the largest creatures I have ever seen — an enormous brown shape, covered in white spots. Its head seemed wider than the boat; its body completely dwarfed our 5-m (18-ft) cabin cruiser. Peter kept the cabin cruiser alongside the whale shark while I donned mask and snorkel, and grabbed my camera. Then, with heart racing, I was over the side for my first underwater encounter with the biggest shark in the ocean.

I snorkelled along next to the whale shark, filled with awe. It seemed unperturbed by my presence, slowly powering itself forward with the side-to-side motion of its tail, and I was able to swim alongside, close enough to touch it. The spots and stripes on its head sparkled in the sunlight. Its mouth seemed to be almost 2 m (6 ft) wide. Up front, a cloud of small fish swam in the pressure wave it created, while under the belly, several suckerfish were hitching a ride — this whale shark was like a moving reef. Along its body there were three prominent ridges, giving it a prehistoric look. The tail was huge — it appeared almost 3 m (10 ft) in height. This creature was truly the master of its environment.

RIDING THE WHALE SHARK

To ride a whale shark is one of the great diving experiences. The diver takes a firm hold of one of the shark's fins and is towed along. As long as the diver's presence is accepted by the shark, the diving 'hitchhiker' can ride along for quite some time. Whale sharks are used to an entourage, frequently being accompanied by a whole assortment of fish. Remoras and slender suckerfish cling to the shark's belly, and some hide in its mouth or its spiracle (a round hole just behind the eyes). A small 'cloud' of juvenile trevally often swim in the pressure wave created in front of the shark. Likewise, large cobia or black kingfish use the shark as a stalking-horse, hiding under it and darting out to attack their prey.

I know of three divers, American friends of mine, who all rode on a whale shark at the same time. The shark was feeding on a 'fishball', a swarm of anchovies, swimming back and forth through the swarm, completely ignoring the three hitchhikers.

There are dangers in riding the sharks — the greatest is being overwhelmed by the excitement of the occasion. Shark expert Dr Eugenie Clark spent several weeks in 1983 searching for whale sharks in the Sea of Cortez, off the west coast of Mexico. When she finally succeeded in diving with one, she stayed with it down to the huge depth of 60 m (185 ft) below the surface. When riding a whale shark, or diving with and photographing one, divers sometimes use snorkelling gear, or they might use scuba-diving equipment. Scuba-diving is much easier with a small, 'pony' scuba tank. The drag of a large tank slows the diver down, making it hard to keep up, but small tanks can also cause problems. *National Geographic* photographer David Doubilet, on one of his first dives at Ningaloo Reef, was using a pony tank when he followed a shark down more than 30 m (100 ft) and found himself running short of air.

My first experience of riding a shark while using scuba-diving equipment was certainly memorable. I took hold of the shark's dorsal fin while still on the surface, at which point it stopped swimming altogether. Then, slowly, we sank to the ocean bottom, 20 m (60 ft) below the surface, with the

BELOW: *A remora hides in the mouth of a whale shark. The whale shark is also known as the rasp-toothed shark 'Rhineodon', as it has several thousand tiny teeth.*

shark rolling gently from side to side; perhaps it was trying to twist around to see me. At the bottom I let go. Realising it was free, the shark swam away, then circled back and swam right up to me, wanting to inspect the intruder, before it powered away.

Riding the whale shark may be exhilarating, but experience soon taught us that many sharks resent the intrusion. For this reason, it became our general policy not to touch or disturb the whale sharks. This requires a certain amount of restraint on the part of divers. (It seems that most people have an irresistible urge to touch wild creatures. Oceanariums often have 'touch pools', where the public can satisfy this desire to handle animals.) These days, riding whale sharks is viewed by many as a form of harassment, and with so many divers visiting Ningaloo, it has now been made illegal in Western Australia.

There are whale sharks of all different sizes at Ningaloo, from small, 3.5-m (12-ft) sharks to giants of up to 10 m (32 ft) long. While there are exceptions to every rule, it has generally been found that only the larger sharks will tolerate being touched. The smaller sharks can object and quickly leave divers who touch them. Put simply, if a shark is left undisturbed, divers can often swim with it for an hour or more, but one diver trying to ride a shark will probably ruin the whole experience for everyone present.

THE DANGERS

There is always the potential for danger when diving in the open sea with whale sharks, but the sharks are rarely the source of this. Particularly in the tropics, there are many creatures that need to be treated with respect.

Sea snakes are common and they can be inquisitive at times. Jellyfish may occasionally be a problem. I've been stung by a large *Tamoya*, which has powerful nematocysts (stinging cells) all over its body. Large stingrays have a huge spine, which can inflict a terrible wound, but they are only encountered on the ocean bottom. They are generally shy, although on one dive in the cold waters of Geographe Bay, a large stingray followed my dive buddy and me for the entire dive. On coral reefs there are other dangers: blue-ringed octopus, stonefish, lionfish and the like. When in the marine environment you soon learn to respect all these creatures, and to leave them alone.

Another source of danger is large, predatory sharks. When diving with whale sharks at Ningaloo Reef, I have occasionally encountered such creatures, but have found them to be far less dangerous than other things.

I remember one occasion when two Oceanic whaler sharks came up from the depths to investigate the group of divers I was with, which included some novice divers. We were in deep water and could not see the bottom. One of the divers panicked, and instead of staying with the group, he sprinted for the boat, which was 200 m (650 ft) away. Thankfully, the Oceanic whaler sharks did not pursue him, but the boat had to stop to pick him up while the rest of us waited with the large sharks circling below us. On another occasion I was swimming with a school of spinner dolphins, trying to photograph them. A sixth sense told me there was something behind me, and sure enough, I looked to find I was being followed by a large tiger shark. I turned to photograph it and it took off into the blue depths below.

There has been at least one instance of a novice aeroplane pilot — who was spotting sharks for a commercial dive boat — directing a boatload of divers to a tiger shark instead of a whale shark. What a shock the divers got. The shark was probably just as surprised, to see several divers swim up to it.

When confronted by a predatory shark, I usually follow the practice that the best way of dealing with such a situation is to remain calm and stand my ground. Sharks are naturally inquisitive, but not normally interested in us as food. One 'amusing' experience illustrates this. I was spearfishing with a friend, Terry Snell, on a patch of fairly shallow limestone reef. I had shot a blue-bone, which had escaped from the spear and hidden in a hole under a ledge on the reef. An injured fish puts out signals that sharks quickly detect. Terry dived down and was hanging upside-down in the water, peering into the darkness under the ledge to locate the fish, when suddenly, a huge shark, about 3 m (10 ft) in length, swam right past me, heading straight for Terry. There was nothing I could do. The shark stopped a few centimetres behind his head. As Terry peered into the darkness under the ledge, the shark tried to get a view over his shoulder, looking first from one side, then the other — it was also after the fish. Unsuccessful, it finally swam off into the gloom. Terry eventually surfaced, completely unaware of the 'comedy' that had taken place. When I told him, he went a whiter shade of pale, and we decided to head for home.

BELOW: *Under a ledge on the reef, a honeycomb cod,* Epinephelus merra, *finds a hole to hide in. A school of golden cardinalfish swim past.*

THE MAN WHO HOOKED A WHALE SHARK

ABOVE: *Sailfish alongside! Exmouth is a major gamefishing centre. Here, a sailfish, caught on light tackle, is brought alongside Danny Driscoll's boat, ready to be tagged and released.*

Game-fishing competitions are taken very seriously in Exmouth: if a whale shark is sighted, game-fishermen circle around with their trolling lines, trying to catch the large cobia that swim alongside the sharks. There is a famous story of two enthusiastic game-fishermen who got more than they bargained for when they succeeded in foul-hooking a whale shark during a competition. Greek fishing identity, Michael Kailis, was on the rod; Italian, Jim Gherardi, owned the boat. Of course, the 10-m (30-ft) whale shark was completely oblivious to the tiny hook, and also to Michael Kailis, straining with all his might to bring it in. Showing typical whale shark curiosity, it obligingly circled round to the back of the 6-m (20-ft) boat and stayed there for a while.

There was great excitement on board. Jim was leaning out of the boat, searching for where the hook had lodged and wondering if he could retrieve his expensive lure. The crew was terrified. Michael was undeterred.

'We've got him! Gaff it! Get the flying gaff', he cried.

'No! Don't be crazy, you'll sink the boat! Cut the b—— line', retorted Jim. He had visions of the entire stern of his old boat falling off if the huge shark was tied off to the stern post.

'No, gaff it! Gaff it! It's a b—— shark! We'll win the competition! It must be a world record', shouted Michael.

'Cut the line! You'll sink the b—— boat', cried Jim. Two of the terrified crew members had also joined in the fray by this time.

Thankfully, the shark took off in the middle of this verbal altercation, breaking the line before either party came to blows.

The whale sharks themselves can also cause the occasional hazardous moment — some of which have their amusing side too. In 1987, American Greg Nelson accompanied a number of divers searching for the sharks. He had heard numerous stories about our encounters and was desperate to experience it for himself. It was an overcast day and very hard to see into the water, making the task of spotting the sharks difficult. Suddenly, we saw a tail cutting through the water close to the boat. If we waited to don scuba gear, we risked losing the shark, so we grabbed masks and fins. Because of the poor visibility, it was hard for Greg to locate the shark as he swung himself over the side to drop feet first into the water. We were in 20 m (60 ft) of water, but Greg got the shock of his life when he found himself standing in water that only came up to his waist: he was standing on the whale shark's head! But only for a moment. The affronted creature took off at high speed; fortunately, Greg was not hit by the tail as it swept past.

Later the same day, Greg followed a whale shark close in to the reef, where the large winter swells were rolling in. I was in the water further offshore, watching as the boat went to pick up Greg — they were just outside the area where the surf breaks against the reef. Suddenly, I was lifted up by a huge swell, and then I watched in horror as it raced on towards the boat. The outboard motor and propeller appeared high in the air as the boat miraculously leapt up, stern first, over the wave. This was one of the first times I'd seen 'king waves' — rogue waves that wash many rock anglers to their deaths every year around the Australian coast.

It was several years before my next encounter with these swells. We had followed a whale shark for more than an hour along the reef, close in to where the surf was breaking, enjoying several dives from the large charter boat. The skipper had stopped to talk to another boat on the radio, when I noticed a 3-m (10-ft) vertical wall of water coming at us from astern. Thankfully, the skipper also saw the wave and powered backwards at full speed just as the wave hit. I ducked under the transom, grabbing the stern rail. Others were taken by surprise as the huge wave broke over the rear deck; a television cameraman and his $70 000 camera were bowled over. For a moment we were awash in 1 m (3 ft) of water, but fortunately, the boat punched through the wave and was not driven onto the reef or broached. Of course we didn't let the skipper forget it for the rest of the trip, asking: 'Aren't we going surfing today?' It is always important to remember that the ocean should not be taken lightly.

Another hazard that the whale sharks present is when they surface directly behind the stern of a boat. These animals are intensely curious, which could be the reason why they do this. I have never seen a whale shark surface behind the stern of a large charter boat, but in the early years when I was searching for them in smaller craft, it happened quite often. Sometimes we would see the sharks trying to swallow the bubbles of exhaust gas coming from the boat's underwater exhaust. Perhaps they thought they were small fish.

But they would also sometimes approach when the motor was cut and the boat was anchored, while we were fishing outside the reef.

On one occasion, I was trying to film American diver Bill Winchester riding on the dorsal fin of a shark. To do this, I needed to get ahead of his bubbles. As we motored up ahead of Bill and the shark, I put on a scuba tank, mask and fins, grabbed the cinecamera, then turned around and leapt clear of the boat. Once airborne, I looked down and was horrified to see a huge white shape in the water directly below me. It was the open mouth of the whale shark. It had come up almost vertically from the bottom to surface immediately behind the stern of the boat. My feet hit the shark, there was a flash of brown as it took off, sideswiping me in the solar plexus with its powerful tail in the process. I was barely able to draw breath. Thankfully the boat was close by.

However, the greatest source of danger when diving with whale sharks is not the sharks themselves, nor other, predatory sharks, nor other sea creatures, but human error. For example, I've had a boat almost reverse over me during one dive. I was waiting to be picked up after diving with a shark,

BELOW: Turquoise Bay — one of the many magnificent, sheltered bays that we used as a base when searching for whale sharks on the trimaran Tribeaut.

and the boat came alongside. As I tried to climb aboard, I realised it was moving backwards — the driver thought the gear lever was in 'neutral', but it had slipped into 'reverse'. A superficial scratch on the thigh from the spinning propeller was my only injury — but it was only a few centimetres away from my femoral artery!

On another occasion at the magnificent Turquoise Bay, I recruited a friend to drive the boat. He had little experience of boats but was keen to see a whale shark. Outside the gap in the reef we soon found one and, grabbing mask and fins, I and another friend jumped overboard. The shark was inquisitive and circled back in our direction. I started filming as it swam towards me. I was looking straight into its mouth — the first frontal head shot I had taken with my new Bolex camera — when suddenly there was a shout, then the boat hit my snorkel, and I turned to see two whirling propellers heading straight for me. I managed to go into a steep dive by pushing off from the bottom of the hull and thus avoided the propellers. I later learnt that the boat driver had been so overwhelmed with excitement at his first sighting of a whale shark that he had left the boat's motor running while he circled around the animal.

THE REWARDS

One of the great pleasures of my involvement with whale sharks has always been to take friends out who have no previous experience of the sharks, or even of diving, and slowly persuade them to enter the water and swim with the huge, gentle creatures. Many of these people would normally never dream of jumping overboard into 20–30 m (60–100 ft) of water, outside the protection offered by the reef, in the habitat of large, predatory sharks. For most of them, the experience was such an exhilarating one that they were on a 'high' for at least a month afterwards.

There was one memorable day in 1986, when the Blinkhorn family accompanied us searching for the sharks. A huge whale shark surfaced at the stern of the boat. It stayed with us for what seemed an eternity. The children were able to lean out from the marlin board and stroke it on the nose. Julia, my eldest child, who was then four years old, swam with me alongside the shark, peering over my shoulder through her small mask at the giant creature a few feet below. Julie Blinkhorn eventually mustered the courage to jump in the water with her daughter Leah, then aged six. Julie tried to stay clear of the business end of the shark — the mouth. However, sensing that something was going on behind it, the shark turned away from the boat and swam up to Julie and Leah. Julie desperately started swimming to get away, but, realising that this was futile, decided to relax and let the shark approach. In her own words, 'I didn't know what to do, so I tickled it under the chin — it seemed to like it'. The huge shark sat there like a baby, almost hypnotised.

BELOW: *A gentle giant.*

Perhaps my most remarkable personal experience with the sharks occurred in 1991, when diving with David Doubilet, photographer, and Eugenie Clark, scientist. David wanted some photos of me with a whale shark, and he wanted something spectacular. As I swam beside a large shark, I started stroking its belly. (I was aware that some animals will go into a trance if their stomach is rubbed.) I gradually moved forward, as it slowed its swimming, until I was beside the mouth, stroking it under the chin. The shark stopped swimming, hanging almost vertically in the water with its mouth close to the surface. For about 20 minutes we stayed there with the shark, stroking it and looking into its cavernous mouth, where a small remora was hiding. We could see every detail of its anatomy, even the sensory electromagnetic pores radiating out from the area beneath the mouth along both sides of the head. In contrast to the tough skin on the shark's back, its belly felt soft, like chamois leather. There we were with one of the largest wild creatures in the world, which was allowing us to caress it in the open sea, seemingly hypnotised. When we eventually left the shark, it slowly swam away.

It is hard to describe the emotions generated by such experiences. Many of the giant creatures in the world have become extinct — some only in recent history. Most of those that remain, such as elephants, rhinoceros, giraffes and large whales, can only be viewed in their natural habitat from a distance. There is no other giant creature on this planet that we can observe and interact with at such close quarters. Perhaps it is this that makes diving with the whale sharks the ultimate diving experience.

ABOVE: *Small schools of juvenile golden trevally,* Gnathanodon speciosus, *often swim in the pressure wave created in front of the whale shark.*

CHAPTER 2

THE BIOLOGY AND ECOLOGY OF THE WHALE SHARK

*J*ust *what is so unique about the whale shark?*

It causes a stir of activity and interest whenever it is

sighted, and yet our knowledge of its biology and habits

is still quite limited. Many people are confused just

by the name — one of the questions I am most often

asked is, is it a whale or a shark?

A WHALE OR A SHARK?

The whale shark *Rhincodon typus* is very much a shark, with very tough skin, gills — like any other fish — five gill slits, and a vertical tail that moves from side to side. It is the largest member of the shark family and as such, the largest fish and the largest cold-blooded animal in the world.

By comparison, whales are mammals, warm-blooded, with skin and hairs, and a huge tail that is horizontal and moves up and down. Whales have lungs, and need to breathe air; they therefore surface every few minutes to take a breath. As they breathe out, the warm air from their lungs condenses in a shower of water vapour — the 'blow' that gives away their location and makes them so vulnerable to whalers.

SCIENTIFIC CLASSIFICATION

The world of fish is divided into the cartilaginous fish, Chondrichthyes, and the bony fish, Osteichthyes. Most of the fish of the reef with which we are familiar are bony fish, that is, covered in scales, with one gill slit on either side of the head. Sharks, skates and rays are different: they are cartilaginous (that is, their skeleton is made of cartilage) and belong to the subclass Elasmobranchii. Three main features distinguish the members of the Elasmobranchii. Their skeleton is made of cartilage; they do not have scales, but instead have hard denticles, which make the skin extremely tough; and they have from five to seven gill slits on each side of the head. Internally, there is another difference: sharks do not have swim bladders to give them buoyancy. The large, oily liver of sharks is thought to help compensate for this lack of an air-filled swim bladder.

There are over 350 identified species of shark in the world. They come in all sorts of shapes and sizes, from the very bizarre goblin sharks (Mitsukurinidae), to the flat, bottom-dwelling angel sharks (Squatinidae) and wobbegongs (Orectolobidae), to the fast-swimming predators with which most of us are familiar. One of the fiercest is the tiny cookie-cutter shark (*Isistius brasiliensis*). Measuring only 50 cm (20 in) in length, it is bold enough to attack large animals such as the baleen whales, using its razor-sharp teeth to gouge the flesh

PREVIOUS PAGE: *A torrent of water pours through this whale shark's gills as it feeds on the surface. This is a rare sight during the daytime at Ningaloo, as the whale sharks seem to prefer to feed from dusk onwards, into the night.*

BELOW: *A tassled wobbegong shark,* Eucrossorhinus dasypogon, *from the family Orectolobidae, hides amongst the coral at Bundegi Reef. This carpet shark, with its broad head, barbels and spiracle, is a close relative of the whale shark.*

from its victims. At the other end of the scale is the whale shark. The largest shark in the ocean, it has tiny, vestigial teeth and is absolutely no threat to other large ocean dwelling creatures (or to humans for that matter). This is because it feeds on some of the smallest creatures to be found in the ocean, the zooplankton.

Sharks are divided into eight orders according to their anatomical make-up. Such features as the presence or absence of an anal fin and the number of gill slits determine their classification. The whale shark fits into the order of Orectolobiformes, which includes species with five gill slits, an anal fin, two dorsal fins, no spines on the fins, and the mouth positioned well in front of the eyes. The word 'orectolobiformes' literally means 'extended tail lobes', and some of the species in the order do have very long tails. They are generally known as the carpet sharks because they are bottom-dwellers. The wobbegong sharks are also members of this order.

Certain features of the whale shark distinguish it from other sharks. The most obvious is its very broad head. Like some carpet sharks — of the Orectolobiformes order — it has a wide mouth that is positioned at the front of the head, rather than on the underside of the head as in other species. The olfactory opening of the whale shark is just above the upper lip, hidden in a nasal groove. There is a small barbel on the inside of this groove, reminiscent of another carpet shark family, the nurse sharks (Ginglymostomatidae).

BELOW: *Carcharias taurus is known in Australia as the grey nurse shark, but elsewhere it is known as the sand tiger shark. It is a large, predatory shark, and is not a member of the nurse shark family. The sensory 'ampullae of Lorenzini', which are a feature of all sharks, can be clearly seen here on its head. The grey nurse shark is much more placid than its vicious appearance would suggest.*

The whale shark's eyes are small and are located behind the angle of the jaw. It does not have any eyelids, but is able to 'close' its eyes by rotating them and sucking them back into its head.

Just behind each of the whale shark's eyes is a round hole called the spiracle. This orifice is a vestigial gill slit, present in many other sharks and rays. It is particularly a feature of carpet sharks. Species with large spiracles are generally bottom-dwellers; rays sometimes respire through the spiracles when resting on the bottom.

Behind the whale shark's spiracles are five large gill slits, their large size being a feature of filter feeders. The gills essentially have two functions — to extract oxygen from the water, and to feed. The whale shark feeds by filtering the small planktonic organisms that are in the water through its five gill slits, which act like sieves.

There are two other distinctive features of the whale shark: it has three prominent ridges along both sides of its body, and its bronze back is patterned with white spots and stripes.

BELOW: *Behind the whale shark's eye is a large hole, the spiracle. This vestigial first gill slit is a feature of bottom-dwelling, or carpet, sharks.*

RHINCODON TYPUS: WHAT'S IN A NAME?

Throughout the history of documenting the whale shark, there has been considerable variation in the spelling of its genus name. The original holotype of the species was described in 1828 under the name *Rhiniodon typus*. 'Rhiniodon' literally means 'rasp tooth'. Over the years, *Rhinodon*, *Rhineodon* and *Rhincodon* have all been used by different authors, and much written on the subject of these name changes. Some authorities (Compagno, 1984) would like to see a return to the original *Rhiniodon typus* rather than the more popular *Rhincodon typus* that is in use currently.

Because of these distinctive features, the whale shark is classified in a family of its own — Rhincodontidae. While some might wonder at the whale shark being grouped with the bottom-dwelling, or carpet, sharks, it has some very obvious features in common with some of these sharks, even though the latter are much smaller. The leopard shark (*Stegostoma fasciatum*), for example, as well as having a large spiracle, also has distinctive ridges along its body and is covered in spots: black spots on a yellow background. The leopard shark is normally a bottom-dwelling shark, but like the whale sharks at Ningaloo, it is sometimes seen basking on the surface.

The nurse sharks also have many similarities, including a nasal groove on the upper jaw that has a prominent barbel. It is thought to have a similar pattern of reproduction, with eggs that are much the same shape as those of the whale shark. (The whale shark's reproductive cycle is discussed in greater detail on page 37.) Indeed, some authorities have suggested that the nurse sharks (Ginglymostomidae) and leopard sharks (Stegastomatidae) should be included in the Rhincodontidae family.

RIGHT: *The gills of the whale shark have two functions — to exchange oxygen and carbon dioxide, and to filter plankton out of the water for food.*

ANATOMY

The dimensions of a really large whale shark are awe-inspiring. The largest specimen ever measured accurately was caught by accident in 1983 off Bombay, India, in a gill net over the side of a 6-m (20-ft) boat. For a while the terrified crew were towed through the water by the shark, which was more than twice the length of the boat. The 12.18 m (40 ft 7 in) male specimen weighed in at 11 tonnes. The mouth was 1.36 m (4½ ft) wide; the dorsal fin was over 1.37 m (4½ ft) high; the pectoral fins, over 2 m (6½ ft) long. An even larger specimen estimated at 18 m (60 ft) in length was reported in the Gulf of Siam in 1925, but its size may have been overestimated (see page 41). This specimen was larger than many of the great whales.

Although it is the largest member of the shark family, the whale shark has very small teeth for its size. Whale sharks vary in this regard from predatory sharks, which are renowned for their large, sharp teeth. Fossils found on old coral reefs at Ningaloo show that these waters were once the home of a predatory monster the same size as the whale shark. *Carcharocles megalodon* (formerly known as *Carcharodon megalodon*) is thought to have become extinct many years ago. Its teeth measured over 8 cm (3 in) in length, twice that of the great white shark — a formidable predator indeed. The whale shark has several thousand teeth, arranged in 11 to 12 rows on the jaw, each tooth being only 2 mm (¹⁄₁₂ in) long and angled back in towards the mouth. The overall appearance is of a large rasp on each jaw. This is the origin of the family name of the whale shark — *Rhinodonte*, the original spelling, means 'rasp tooth'. It is thought that the harsh noise sometimes heard by pearl fishers underwater when a whale shark is close by could be produced by the sharks grinding their teeth together.

The whale shark rarely uses its teeth however, and certainly not when feeding. It uses its five gill slits, which have fine gill rakers, to filter small planktonic organisms out of the water. This is known as filter feeding.

The whale shark is one of three species of sharks — all massive — that are filter feeders. The others are the basking shark (*Cetorhinus maximus*) and the megamouth shark (*Megachasma pelagios*). The basking shark is a grey-coloured shark with a pointed nose that lives in more temperate seas. It grows to a length of 9 m (30 ft) and has very large gill slits. It cruises at the surface with its mouth gaping, filtering the water with its gill rakers. The megamouth shark is an elusive creature, mainly known because of dead specimens being periodically washed up onshore. Growing to at least 4.5 m (15 ft) long, it is thought to be a filter feeder, although it has larger teeth than the other two species and does not have their huge gill slits.

The gill slits of the whale sharks are relatively large, in keeping with this method of feeding — only the basking shark has bigger gills. And yet what is remarkable is that the whale shark is believed to be able to filter prey only 1 mm (¹⁄₂₄ in) in diameter. When actively feeding, it pumps large volumes of water through the gills at speed, causing the gills to flare out.

There is still some confusion about the actual filter-feeding method of the whale shark, and at Ningaloo it has been seen feeding in different ways. Traditionally, the whale shark is described as a suction filter feeder. By suddenly opening its mouth, it is able to draw a large volume of water inside, which it then expels through the gill slits. In the normal process of respiration, the whale shark rhythmically opens its mouth about 20 cm (8 in) wide. When feeding, it is able to open its mouth two to three times wider. Sometimes the shark feeds passively, cruising along beneath the surface with mouth agape, feeding in the same manner as the basking shark. At other times it feeds much more actively, charging around on the surface, as when attacking a swarm of tropical krill (*Pseudeuphausia latifrons*).

The internal organs of the whale shark have rarely been examined by marine biologists, as most of the specimens that have come to scientific

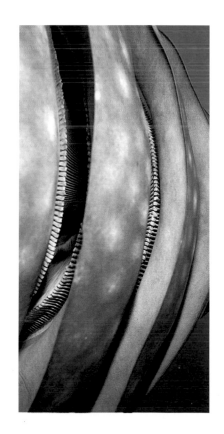

BELOW: *Close up of the gill slits — the whale shark is thought to be able to filter prey as small as 1 mm (¹⁄₂₄ in) in diameter through these.*

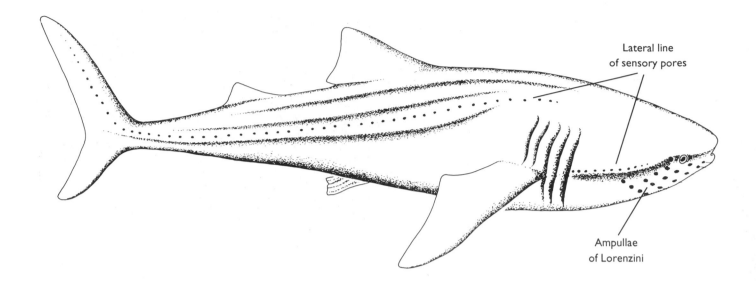

Lateral line
of sensory pores

Ampullae
of Lorenzini

ABOVE: *The lateral line of sensory pores detects low-level vibrations. The electromagnetic sensory pores around the head, known as the 'ampullae of Lorenzini', are used by the whale shark to detect electromagnetic fields in the water and to locate prey.*

attention have rapidly putrefied. The shark is believed to have a small gullet, and while it may be able to take large objects into its mouth, it is unable to swallow them. The liver of the shark is huge — in a 12-m (40-ft) shark, the liver alone weighs 1 tonne, 9 per cent of its total body weight. Extracts of the whale shark's liver are reported to have strong anti-tumour properties.

The skin on the back of the whale shark is thicker and tougher than that of any other species in the world. The outer layer is covered in overlapping dermal denticles, a veritable suit of armour. Each denticle is 0.5 mm wide, and 0.75 mm long. The point of each denticle is shaped backwards along the body. Underneath this layer is a layer of connective tissue that can be up to 14 cm (5½ in) thick. The belly of the shark is much softer and the thickness of the connective tissue in this area is only two-thirds the thickness of that on the back. It is interesting to note that when swimming past divers, the sharks often 'bank' onto their sides to present their tough dorsal skin to the diver, rather than their soft underbelly.

Sharks are believed to have extraordinary powers of healing. There is evidence of this in the whale sharks at Ningaloo. A whale shark filmed in 1986 had two deep gashes down one side of its body. It was easily identifiable because of an old shark 'bite' in its left pectoral fin, scars on its flank, and its lateral markings. When sighted again in 1993, the two gashes had completely healed, without any scarring whatsoever.

The whale shark's eyes are relatively small for a creature that spends much of its life in the dark depths of the ocean, suggesting that eyesight is not an important sense. It would certainly find it difficult to locate its tiny prey using eyesight alone.

Some sharks have an extremely sensitive sense of smell, and studies have been made of chemicals that attract and repel sharks. Sharks often forage and feed at night when vision is of little use, and the ability to detect chemicals in the water is therefore thought to be of paramount importance to sharks when locating their locating prey. The nasal grooves above the mouth of particular sharks, including the whale shark, enable a continuous stream of water to flow past their olfactory apparatus.

Probably the most important sense, however, is the puzzling sixth sense. Like other species of shark, the whale shark has a very definite lateral line of sensory 'pores', where their vibration sensory system is located. The pores of the lateral line can clearly be identified along the body of the whale shark below the second longitudinal ridge in the third depression. The lateral line starts at the tip of the dorsal fin of the tail, passes down either side of this fin to the tail peduncle, and then it travels along both sides of the body in the third depression between the ridges. It then rises up over the dorsum of

the gill slits and passes onto the top of the head. Further lines of pores can be seen in front of the shark's gills. Around the shark's head there are larger pores, known as the 'ampullae of Lorenzini'. These pores make up the electromagnetic sensory system, which is capable of detecting changes in magnetic fields as well as the minute electrical currents generated by the movement of fish.

ABOVE: *Three lateral ridges run down either side of the whale shark's body. The lateral line of sensory pores runs the length of the body in the depression between the second and third ridges.*

HABITAT

The whale shark has been found in all the major oceans, but appears not to enter the Mediterranean Sea. It lives in the warm waters of tropical and subtropical seas. Its range extends further towards the poles on the eastern coasts of continents, where warm tropical waters are carried away from the equator by ocean currents. Thus, on the east coast of Australia, the whale shark has been sighted as far south as Point Hicks in Victoria, which is below latitude 38° south. Similarly, the sharks have been seen off Cape Town in South Africa. In the northern hemisphere, whale sharks are carried north by the warm Kuroshio Current to the islands of southern Japan and by the Gulf Stream on

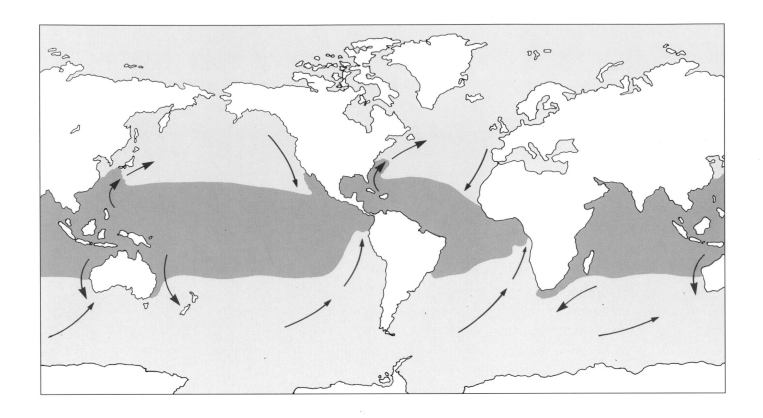

ABOVE: *The distribution of whale sharks throughout the world correlates with water warmer than 20°C (68°F). This is also the distribution of coral reefs. The arrows indicate the flow of the world's ocean currents. (After Wolfsen, 1986)*

the east coast of North America. In Western Australia they have been sighted as far south as the Kalbarri Cliffs, at latitude 28° south.

It is not known how far whale sharks migrate. At one time it was suggested that they might undertake huge migrations, which involved breeding in the Indian Ocean, then drifting south in the Mozambique Current, around Cape Horn into the Atlantic Ocean, across which they might then be carried by the Southern Equatorial Current to the Caribbean (Gudger, 1931). Diver and film-maker Ben Cropp believes the whale sharks on the east coast of Australia undertake an annual migration. He believes that, starting from south-eastern New Guinea, where large numbers of whale sharks have been seen in September, they travel south along the Great Barrier Reef and appear off the Capricorn Group, off the central Queensland coast, in November and early December after the annual coral spawning has taken place. Some of them continue south, being sighted off the Gold Coast in January, and off New South Wales in March and April. Studies at Ningaloo Reef to date do not support a major migration (see page 126).

Whale sharks prefer waters with a surface temperature of 21°–26°C (70°–79°F), in areas where there are upwellings of nutrient-rich colder water. These conditions favour the blooms of plankton on which the sharks feed. They are often seen with schools of pelagic fish, especially trevally or jacks. (More information about the feeding practices of the whale shark can be found on pages 131–2.)

REPRODUCTION AND LIFE CYCLE

The method of reproduction of the whale shark is a mystery that continues to keep scientists guessing. If you open up a mature, dead female whale shark, the uterus may be full of large eggs, similar to the eggs of dogfish that have been found washed up on beaches, but much larger. One such egg containing a baby shark 35.5 cm (14½ in) long was brought up in a trawl net in the Gulf of Mexico in 1953. It was caught by Captain Odell Freeze, fishing out of Port Isabel, Texas. He could feel that something was kicking inside the egg and, upon opening it with his knife, found a baby whale shark, very much alive.

This egg has stimulated much discussion among marine biologists. At the time it seemed to prove that the whale shark is oviparous, producing eggs that hatch outside the mother's body, laying them on the ocean floor. If this is so, however, why are the eggs not frequently washed up on beaches throughout the tropics? The similarities between the whale shark and other carpet sharks have already been discussed (see pages 29, 31). Some carpet sharks, such as the leopard shark, are known to be egg-laying species, whereas others, such as the nurse sharks, give birth to live young.

It now seems more likely that the whale shark is ovo-viviparous, that is, the newborn sharks hatch out of the eggs while inside the body of the mother and are then expelled from her. Newborn whale sharks have been caught in the Persian Gulf, the Gulf of Guinea in the Atlantic Ocean, and in the Pacific Ocean, off the Central American coast. They have ranged from 55–63 cm (21–25 in) in length. Whale sharks measuring from 3.5 m (11½ ft) upwards have been caught around the world, but there had been no reports of whale sharks between 1 and 3.5 m (3 and 11½ ft) long until scientists were called to investigate a strange phenomenon in the Sea of Cortez, off Mexico, in 1993, where small sharks were annoying local fishermen. The sharks were feeding on the surface, their large mouths agape. They were so intent on feeding that they frequently bumped into the sides of the fishing boats. They turned out to be juvenile whale sharks, about 3 m (10 ft) in length, and they were feeding on the rich zooplankton in the area.

The life expectancy of many species of sharks is not known. However, most species that have been studied live for at least 15 years. The white-spotted dogfish is known to live for more than 100 years, and it does not reach sexual maturity until it is 20 years of age. Hence these sharks must spend almost one-fifth of their lives escaping capture before they are able to reproduce at all.

The longevity of the whale shark is not yet known, although its life pattern is thought to be similar to that of the white-spotted dogfish. Preliminary evidence at Ningaloo Reef appears to indicate that the male whale shark does not reach sexual maturity until 30 years of age (see page 139). If, as with the dogfish, this is less than one-fifth its life expectancy, then it is not unlikely that the whale shark may be one of the longest living creatures on earth. Further study will resolve this and some of the other mysteries surrounding the animal.

ABOVE: A 'mermaid's purse'. Shark eggs such as this small specimen are found washed up on beaches throughout the world. The whale shark's egg is similar in appearance, although larger.

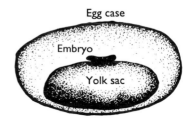

BELOW: Cross-section of a typical shark egg. Whether the whale shark is an egg-laying species, or whether it gives birth to live young, is still not known with certainty. However, based on sightings of newborn whale sharks in various parts of the world, the latter now seems more likely.

Egg case

Embryo

Yolk sac

CHAPTER 3

THE STRANGE HISTORY OF THE WHALE SHARK

Enormous, and yet elusive — it's hardly surprising that the whale shark is surrounded by myth and mystery. Scientific investigations began in the early 1800s, and in the last 40 years, the whale shark has been more widely documented, helping to dispel some of the strangeness that surrounds it.

A CREATURE
OF FEAR AND SUPERSTITION

The sight of a shark 12 m (40 ft) long must have struck terror into the hearts of early seafarers and fishermen. They were by nature superstitious, and only too aware of the dangers of the ocean environment. Even a gentle creature such as the giant manta ray was named the 'devil ray' by early seafarers.

Such impressions were largely engendered by early lithographs of sea monsters, drawn by artists with vivid imaginations, based on the exaggerated descriptions of seafarers. In ancient history descriptions can be found of 'sea monsters' devouring seafarers as their ships sank. One of the earliest documented shark attacks took place in 1580 on a voyage from Portugal to India. A sailor who had fallen overboard had been thrown a rope and was being hauled back into the boat, when a large monster appeared from the depths and tore him to pieces before the other sailors' eyes. Stories such as this one caused a great fear of the deep, as well as some very strange ideas on the part of seafaring people. Even during my youth, many professional fishermen on the north-east coast of England believed it was better not to be able to swim: if your boat sank, it was considered better to drown quickly than to die a lingering death or risk being torn to pieces by sharks. It's not difficult to imagine that for early sailors and anglers, the whale shark, with its enormous proportions, would truly have been a monster of the deep.

Some experts consider that the monster that swallowed Jonah in the biblical story was in fact a shark rather than a whale. And if it was a shark, surely it must have been a whale shark. In the original Hebrew version of this story, the word used is 'tanninum', which means a large sea animal. Although the great white shark has been known to swallow a sailor whole, it is very unlikely that anyone would survive the experience of being ripped to pieces by its teeth on entry, let alone on exit. The whale shark is the only species that really fits the bill.

PREVIOUS PAGE: Jonah and the Great Fish. Many experts believe that the sea monster of the biblical story may well have been a shark. If so, it must have been a whale shark.

BELOW: A medieval artist's impression of the sea monsters to be found lurking in the dark depths of the ocean.

DOCUMENTED BY SCIENTISTS

The first whale shark specimen known to scientists was captured in Table Bay on the Cape of Good Hope (near what is now Cape Town, South Africa) in 1828. This is at the southernmost limit of their distribution, where the Mozambique Current brings warm tropical water down the east coast of Africa. The small shark, a mere 4.6 m (15 ft 4 in) long, was caught with a harpoon. Andrew Smith, an English doctor in Cape Town at the time, recorded that 'when approached, it manifested no great degree of fear, and it was not before a harpoon was lodged in its body that it altered its course and quickened its pace'. The specimen was purchased for £6 by a Mr J. Verreaux, who organised to have it preserved and sent to the Paris Museum. A description of it featured in Smith's account of the natural history of South Africa, published in 1829 in the *Zoological Journal*. It is the original holotype specimen used to define the species and, remarkably, it still exists today in the Musée National d'Histoire Naturelle in Paris, although it is currently not on display.

In 1865 Mr A. Dumeril published his *Histoire Naturelle des Poissons ou Ichthyologie Générale*, which included an entry for the whale shark under the name *Rhinodon typicus* and a detailed description of the Paris Museum's specimen. He described this specimen as 'the only known example of this species'.

However, in the same year, 1865, another specimen was caught, in the Gulf of California. A second American specimen was later recorded found in Panama Bay, off the coast of Panama, in 1884.

Historically, the largest specimen reported in the scientific literature was an animal that in 1919 became trapped in the entrance of a bamboo stake-trap set in water 14.5–16 m (48–54 ft) deep off Koh Chik (Chik Island) in what was then known as the Gulf of Siam (now the Gulf of Thailand). It remained stuck there for seven days and was then killed with rifle bullets. It was so huge that the fishermen were unable to haul it ashore. No measurements were taken, but it was estimated to be 10 *wa*. The *wa* was the Siamese fathom, and represented the full reach of a man's outstretched arms. The Siamese were not a tall race, and it is therefore unlikely that a *wa* measured more than 1.5–1.6 m (5–5½ ft). Hugh Smith, who wrote a report of this event in 1925, suggested the *wa* would be equivalent to a span of 1.7–1.8 m (5⅔–6 ft), but in my view, this was probably an overestimate. However, even if the trapped animal was 15 m (50 ft) long, it would have been a formidable size, and bigger than any whale shark that has been accurately measured.

The Gulf of Mexico, off the United States coast, was another region where whale sharks were frequently sighted in the early part of this century. In 1923, a Mr I. W. Wallace reported that a very large whale shark was often seen, which appeared to be longer than a 23-m (76-ft) fishing vessel, the *Hays*. The shark was nicknamed 'Big Ben', and it was reported that men occasionally jumped overboard and walked on its back.

ABOVE: *Dr Eugene Gudger, a Curator of Fishes at the American Museum of Natural History, collected reports of whale sharks from all over the world from 1915 to the 1950s.*

Two scientists working during the 20th century were to devote their lives to studying the whale shark. The first, Dr Eugene W. Gudger, was born in 1866 in Waynesville, North Carolina. He completed two degrees, including a Ph.D. degree at Johns Hopkins University, and taught for many years. It was not until 1919 that he took up a position at the American Museum of Natural History, where he was later to become a Curator of Fishes and the world's leading authority on whale sharks.

From 1913 to 1953, Gudger published 47 papers on the species. He collected reports from all over the world about whale sharks that had been harpooned, stranded on beaches, or impaled on the bows of large ships. It seems that whale sharks were frequently caught across the bows of ships earlier this century, trapped by the bulbous 'nose' of the bow under water. One ship, the *President Wilson*, struck sharks in the Red Sea in two consecutive years, 1936 and 1937. In order to release the sharks, it was necessary to stop the ship and then to reverse. Sometimes the sharks were so badly injured that they were dead by the time they were released. It is interesting to note that these reports of impalings on the bows of ships seem to have ceased. Observers have commented that the reason for this may be that the sharks are getting rarer.

Gudger claimed to have a copy of every whale shark photo ever taken in the early days of the century. In one of his papers, 'The Whale Shark Unafraid', Gudger (1941) examined all the known accounts of human contact with the whale shark, concluding that '*Rhineodon typus* fears not shark, man nor ship'. He also collected some remarkable anecdotes, including the first sighting of a whale shark ever to gain Western attention, which occurred in 1816, near Manila, in the Philippines. A huge shark passed under an anchored vessel, making it appear that the vessel was adrift over the coral; the crew thought the anchor had parted. It was also reported that in the Philippines the fishermen feared the whale shark, which, it was alleged, had attacked fishing boats, and on one occasion had swallowed a man who had fallen overboard. However, the whale shark seemed to have a benign reputation elsewhere in the tropics. There were frequent reports of fishermen harpooning the sharks, while from the Seychelles came the report of one particular danger: if a harpooned whale shark sounded (that is, went into a sudden, rapid dive) and the rope attached to the harpoon was too short, the shark could pull the pirogue (a type of fishing vessel) and crew to the bottom.

In June 1923, a 9.5-m (32-ft) whale shark was harpooned off the Florida Keys, in the United States, and towed to the port of Marathon, where it died two days later. The captors donated the specimen to the American Museum of Natural History. Unfortunately, the animal began decomposing while being towed from Marathon to Key West, Florida Keys, but photographs and measurements taken of the animal nevertheless allowed Gudger to construct a scale model of the shark at the Museum. It was 9.5 m (32 ft) long, and the circumference behind the eyes was 4 m (14 ft). The largest circumference measured 7 m (23 ft), behind the pectoral fins. The tail was 3.5 m (12 ft) tall.

The American Museum of Natural History was not the only museum to have a display of this 'monster of the deep'. There was the 1829 specimen caught in Table Bay, South Africa, which had been sent to the Paris Museum, and the Colombo Museum in Ceylon (now Sri Lanka) also had a whale shark on display, by 1883, and in 1889 it sent a specimen to the British Museum.

LEFT: *Reports of whale sharks being impaled on the bows of large ships were common during the early part of this century. This small whale shark collided with the S.S. Francesco Crispi in the Indian Ocean in 1932.*

The other major whale shark expert was Dr Fay Wolfson, of the Hubbs Marine Research Institute in San Diego, United States. Like Gudger, she documented reports of the sharks from all over the world, and published a bibliography of the sharks (Wolfson and Notarbartolo di Sciari, 1981). Her greatest contribution, however, was to collate all the 320 sightings of the sharks that had been reported in the Western scientific literature up until 1987 — surely a measure of the rarity of the species. Unlike her predecessor Gudger, Wolfson was to see a live whale shark: when she travelled to Okinawa, Japan, she viewed a captive whale shark in an aquarium. Later, she travelled to the Sea of Cortez, hoping to see a whale shark in the wild. Dr Eugenie Clark, a world authority on sharks, was there at the same time, on a similar quest. Eugenie tells the story of their meeting:

> *We were making a movie for ABC–TV from another dive boat, the* Don José. *Stan Waterman, Howard Hall, Peter Benchly and I figured we had a 50–50 chance of seeing a whale shark. We had a spotter plane to help us try to locate one. Each evening we anchored near Fay's group [on the boat* Floradora] *led by famous cinematographer, Jack McKenny. We were all having great dives on the sea mount [an underwater sea mountain] with manta rays, hammerhead sharks, and the marvellous concentration of fishes that live on sea mounts. Finally, after five days of waiting, we saw one. That evening after filming a big female that I rode on down to 185 ft [55 m], I visited the* Floradora *to see Fay. I was so thrilled and excited, but as I started to tell her about our wonderful adventure, I curtailed it as I saw a mixture of awe and pain in her expression. 'You'll dive with one in the next few days', I assured her. But they finally left without this ultimate dive experience.*

It is sadly ironic that the world's two greatest whale shark aficionados, Gudger and Wolfson, both died without ever having sighted a live whale shark in the wild. And Wolfson never knew about Ningaloo Reef. Learning of her work on the sharks, I wrote to her in 1989, hoping to interest her in research collaboration. I received no reply, and it was only much later that I learnt of her premature death from cancer in the late 1980s.

Dr Eugenie Clark, Senior Research Scientist and Professor Emeritus of the University of Maryland, has since taken up the whale shark cause. Eugenie was a pioneer of shark research, opening her own marine laboratory at Cape Haze, Florida, in 1955. She enlisted the help of local shark fishermen to catch sharks so that she could study their anatomy and their behaviour. With a grant received in the late 1950s, she built a boat to help in the pursuit of her shark studies — appropriately, the boat was called *Rhincodon*. Eugenie has dived with and researched sharks all over the world, but it was not until the late 1970s that she first had the thrill of diving with whale sharks in the Sea of Cortez. In 1991 she came to Western Australia to see first hand the whale shark phenomenon of Ningaloo Reef.

POPULARISED BY FILMS AND BOOKS

It seems remarkable that the first underwater film footage of the whale shark was taken as early as 1926. Mack Sennett, an American motion picture producer, managed to film a whale shark while on a fishing trip to Cape San Lucas, on the southern tip of the Baja California peninsula, in Mexico. A copy of the film was presented to the American Museum of Natural History.

However, it was the black and white films of Hans and Lottie Hass shown on television during the 1950s that first brought the underwater world into living rooms throughout the Western world. Hans Hass was the first photographer to film the whale shark in the Red Sea. It was in 1950, while he was searching for manta rays. The shark was 7.5 m (25 ft) long, and Hass went for a ride on its dorsal fin, then attempted to ride its tail. There can be little doubt that the exciting adventures recorded by the Hasses inspired many, including myself, to take to the water in search of adventure.

BELOW: *Shafts of silver light accentuate the ridges along this shark's body. These ridges give the whale sharks an almost prehistoric appearance — they have always reminded me of dinosaurs.*

A VERITABLE SEA MONSTER

Many people would have first read about the whale shark in Thor Heyerdahl's book, *The Kon-Tiki Expedition* (1950). There, it is described as having 'the biggest and ugliest face any of us had ever seen in the whole of our lives'. Heyerdahl continues:

BELOW: *To some, a veritable monster.*

BOTTOM: *A 'sharke fish', an early sea monster.*

It was the head of a veritable sea monster, so huge and hideous that if the Old Man of the Sea himself had come up he could not have made such an impression on us. The head was broad and flat like a frog's, with two small eyes right at the sides, and a toadlike jaw which was four or five feet [1–1.5 m] wide and had long fringes hanging from the corners of the mouth.

A veritable monster indeed! This is certainly the least flattering account of whale sharks in any literature.

Perhaps it is a testament to the rarity of the whale shark that the Cousteau family — internationally famous for capturing on film the underwater worlds of many different sea creatures — in all their early years of cruising the oceans, only ever encountered two. In 1967, while travelling up the east coast of Africa on the *Calypso*, they suddenly spotted the dorsal fins of a whale shark estimated at 10.5 m (35 ft) long. Soon after, a second shark was sighted, thought to be well over 12 m (40 ft) long. The water that day was so full of plankton that 'it resembled a gigantic bowl of hot soup'. There was great excitement as a group of divers dived with these giants, and they were particularly impressed with the way the sharks sounded — 'going straight down on a vertical line'.

Ben Cropp was the first person to film whale sharks in Australia. In 1965, he took footage of a whale shark that had been sighted regularly by divers and anglers off Montague Island, New South Wales. This island, which is below latitude 36° south, is at the extreme southerly limit of the whale sharks' range. Ben Cropp's 16-mm film footage was blown up and published in magazines throughout the world, further bringing the whale shark to the attention of the general public.

ABOVE: *Diver and film-maker Ben Cropp first filmed whale sharks off the New South Wales coast in 1965. Ben believes the sharks found on the east coast of Australia migrate from New Guinea.*

THE MYSTERY OF MINI

One fascinating whale shark story from 1976 involves a female whale shark that became trapped in the lagoon of Canton Island, an atoll in the Phoenix group, in the central Pacific Ocean. The shark appeared to be lost in a small pond, amid a maze of channels between the coral outcrops. Attempts were made by the local people to get her through a channel into the main lagoon, using nets, but they were unsuccessful. However, they were successful in feeding her on a diet of shrimps, and the shark soon learnt to come to a small skiff to be fed, repeatedly thrusting her open mouth out of the water against the skiff. She eventually found her way to the lagoon.

'Mini', as she was nicknamed, stayed in the lagoon and was fed for over 14 months. Presumably, she eventually escaped to the open sea, for one day, she disappeared. Her story is yet another testament to the remarkable nature of this gentle giant.

CHAPTER 4

NINGALOO REEF AND NORTH-WEST CAPE

Ningaloo Reef is situated off the remote North-West Cape — a place that very few people have ever seen. The reef has an abundance of marine life. There are the whale sharks, as well as fish of all shapes and colours, dolphins, dugongs, giant whales, predatory sharks, and brilliant corals. This abundance is in dramatic contrast to the stark and arid beauty of the Cape itself.

CLIMATE

Ningaloo Reef is to be found on the west coast of the North-West Cape peninsula. The Cape juts out northwards like a finger into the Indian Ocean on the west coast of Western Australia, crossing the Tropic of Capricorn and reaching latitude 21°53 south. This is the Trade Wind belt, and the prevailing south-easterly winds bring hot, dry winds from the centre of the continent. The summer temperature frequently climbs over the 38°C (100°F) mark. As the land heats up, convection currents suck in the cooling sea-breezes off the ocean, bringing relief from the scorching heat.

This is the latitude of deserts throughout the world. The coastal region averages only 250 mm (10 in) of rain each year. In some years the rain is brought by summer cyclones, but these are very unpredictable and often pass by the Cape, well out to sea. More reliable are the winter tropical convergences, when warm tropical air, streaming southwards, converges on cooler air that is coming up from the south. The resulting condensation causes thick bands of cloud that stream across the whole continent in early winter (May to July), often bringing torrential rain to the dry coastal and inland areas.

In Australia, weather systems generally arrive from the west. It is therefore difficult to imagine that the weather changes in the eastern Pacific have a major influence on Australian weather and rainfall levels. Scientists have studied the 'El Niño' phenomenon, which is also known as the 'Southen Oscillation', hoping that it will enable them to predict the pattern of cyclones that affect the north of Australia and the western Pacific. In years of strong El Niño effect, the sea-water temperature rises 2°–4°C (3.5°–7°F) off the coast

BELOW: Satellite photo of the North-West Cape peninsula. The pale blue area indicates the reef offshore, while Ningaloo Marine Park is the area between the coast and the white line. The extensive mangrove systems of Exmouth Gulf are also visible.

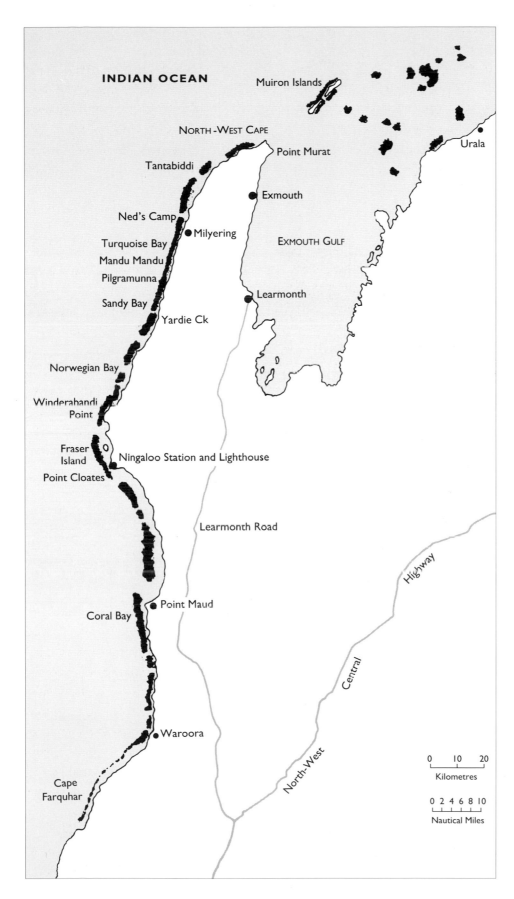

INDIAN OCEAN

Muiron Islands

NORTH-WEST CAPE

Point Murat

Urala

Tantabiddi

Exmouth

Ned's Camp

Milyering

Turquoise Bay

EXMOUTH GULF

Mandu Mandu

Pilgramunna

Sandy Bay

Learmonth

Yardie Ck

Norwegian Bay

Winderabandi Point

Fraser Island

Ningaloo Station and Lighthouse

Point Cloates

Learmonth Road

Highway

Coral Bay

Point Maud

Central

Waroora

North-West

Cape Farquhar

0 10 20
Kilometres

0 2 4 6 8 10
Nautical Miles

LEFT: *The North-West Cape region and Ningaloo Reef.*

PREVIOUS PAGES (PAGES 48–9): *'Ningaloo' is the local Aboriginal name for this promontory, now known as Point Cloates, which lies at the very heart of Ningaloo Reef. The lighthouse still stands on the dunes, and Ningaloo pastoral station lies just to the north-west. It was here that the story of my quest for the whale sharks started.*

of Ecuador and Peru. This affects the temperature and the flow of the equatorial sea currents travelling west towards Australia.

One thing that has become clear is that in years of strong El Niño effect, summer storm cells persist off the northern coast of Australia into early winter, bringing heavy winter rainfall. In the years 1983, 1987 and 1992, the region enjoyed heavy winter rains that transformed the arid desert into a garden. The El Niño effect is so powerful that it also affects the strength of the sea currents flowing on the west coast, and indirectly influences such things as the breeding of rock lobsters and the productivity of offshore fisheries.

THE GEOLOGY OF NORTH-WEST CAPE

The backbone of the Cape peninsula is a range of hills that rises in a steep escarpment on the west coast (the Indian Ocean side) and slopes more gently towards Exmouth Gulf in the east. The sandstone and limestone beds that make up this range were laid down in relatively recent geological time, on the ocean floor, with the oldest beds being about 30 million years old. Titanic geological forces, caused by moving tectonic plates, have pushed these beds up into a huge anticline, which now rises over 300 m (1000 ft) high. This is thought to have occurred between 1.6 and 5 million years ago. Between 10 000 years and

RIGHT: *Torrential cyclonic rains have carved steep-sided gorges in the soft limestone of the Cape Range anticline.*
BELOW: *Trumpet and baler shells embedded in the floor of a cave, close to the town of Exmouth, indicate that the area was under the ocean in relatively recent geological times.*

1.6 million years ago, the sea level varied greatly, being low during the Ice Ages and high during the interglacial periods. As the sea receded, old coral reefs were left 'stranded' onshore. Subjected to torrential, cyclonic rains, the ranges have been cut by steep-sided gorges and riddled with underground caves.

The underground caves harbour the bones of some mammals that are now extinct. In two caves, bones of the Tasmanian tiger (*Thylacinus cynocephalus*) have been found, indicating that this species, long extinct on the mainland and possibly extinct in Tasmania, once roamed across the whole of the Australian continent. Unique species of troglobites have also been observed in the caves. Many are crustaceans such as amphipods and shrimps. Other troglobites include the rare schizomids and pseudoscorpions, types of arachnid related to spiders and scorpions.

The limestone of the Cape is like a sponge, riddled with holes — below the water table it forms a huge, interconnecting aquifer system. On the flat coastal plains of the Cape there are caves known as 'namma holes'. These holes in the limestone bedrock open into systems of subterranean caves, which provide access to underground pools of water below the level of the water table. Living in perpetual darkness, the creatures that inhabit this world of the underground — fish, eels and shrimps — have no need of eyes and they have therefore evolved without them. Neither do they have any pigment in their skin. One species, the blind gudgeon *Milyeringa veritas*, is a common sight in many of the underground waterholes around the Cape. At the other extreme, the blind eel *Opisternum candidum* is so rare that only two have been seen by cavers in ten years.

BELOW: *The sun streams into Owls Roost Cave, a cave typical of the Cape Range, where owls have brought the bones of small animals. As with many caves in the region, a fig tree grows out of the entrance.*

ABOVE: *A tooth of the extinct* Carcharocles megalodon, *found by my daughter Julia in 1990, in a terrace of the rock strata of the Cape Range.*

BELOW: *A Brahminy kite,* Haliastur indus, *watches for prey.*

In one cave discovered in 1993 on the coastal plain close to the town of Exmouth (on the east coast of the Cape), hundreds of large shells were found. These shells prove that in relatively recent geological times, the coastal plain was flooded and these caves were under the ocean.

As the Cape Range was lifted out of the ocean, the wave action of the sea cut terraces in the rock strata along the west coast. Some of the rock outcrops on the coastal plains are old reefs where fossilised shells can be found, and the teeth of one of the largest sharks that ever lived, the massive *Carcharocles megalodon*. This huge predatory shark was as big as a whale shark, and had teeth two to three times the size of those of the largest great white sharks alive today. *Carcharocles megalodon* lived from the Miocene to the late Pliocene epochs (2.3–1.6 million years ago), and the finding of these teeth has rewritten the geological history of this area. The terraces where they were found are now thought to be at least 1.6 million years old.

To the east of the Cape Range are the waters of Exmouth Gulf, and to the south, beds of rock formed during the Cretaceous period (65–146 million years ago) are exposed. Here are fossil remains of many marine creatures that are the ancestors of modern marine life. Ammonites, bivalves and brachiopods are common, and amongst them are numerous small sharks' teeth, indicating that sharks were swimming in the oceans of this area 80 million years ago.

FLORA AND FAUNA OF THE CAPE

The hot, dry climate of the Cape has produced a harsh environment of stunted acacia shrubs struggling to survive amid the rocks and spinifex grasses. The coastal plain is the home to a large population of red kangaroos and euro kangaroos. Emus are also common. They will stroll down the main street of Exmouth, searching for food — the dates on the palms are a favourite.

The foothills of the ranges are home to the black-footed rock wallaby — a large colony can be found on the rock walls of the beautiful Yardie Creek Gorge. Like many Australian marsupials, this charming little wallaby hides in caves during the day, emerging late in the afternoon to forage around the gorge. Its survival is threatened by introduced species such as feral cats and foxes.

For bird enthusiasts the Cape has many species of interest, the most spectacular of all being the large raptors. The sea eagle and the osprey are frequently seen along the coast. Sadly, the presence of people forced the ospreys to move their nests to the offshore islands, although deserted nests can still be found in several sites around the Cape. Their frequent attempts to nest on telecommunications towers have been prevented; however, one pair has nested on the Naval Jetty at Point Murat since 1992. The waters under the jetty are full of fish and they have had prodigious breeding success. Their young can frequently be observed here. While boating around the Cape, it is easy to spot ospreys fishing, diving out of the sky to grab a fish from the surface of the ocean.

Other raptors are commonly seen: eagles, ranging from the little eagle to the huge wedge-tailed eagle; the black-shouldered kite; and the larger goshawk, one of the fastest flyers in the sky. In the heat of summer, the hawks often fly around Exmouth, where water is more plentiful. Some of them succumb to heat stress.

On the tidal flats of the Cape, within Exmouth Gulf, there are many varieties of waders and terns, which migrate through the area. Godwits from Siberia are common visitors. Offshore, flocks of wedge-tailed shearwaters and terns can be seen following schools of tuna. The small, black and white terns glint in the sunlight. The white-winged black terns are winter visitors from Asia. After summer cyclones, some unexpected visitors can appear: black frigate birds are occasionally seen on the west coast of the Cape, most likely strays from Christmas Island, more than 2200 km (1320 miles) away.

BELOW: *The rich ochre colour of limestone rock walls, reflected in the waters of Yardie Creek, an oasis created by the year-round flooding of Yardie Creek Gorge.*

NATIONAL PARKS OF NORTH-WEST CAPE

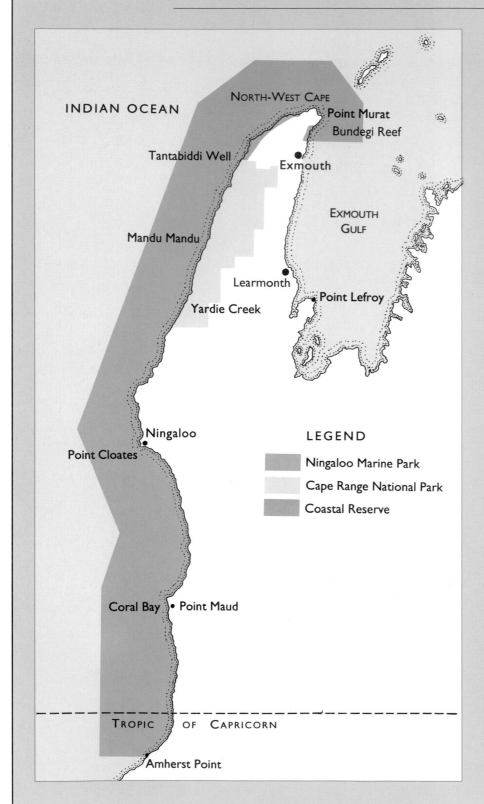

INDIAN OCEAN

NORTH-WEST CAPE

Point Murat
Bundegi Reef

Tantabiddi Well

Exmouth

EXMOUTH GULF

Mandu Mandu

Learmonth

Point Lefroy

Yardie Creek

Ningaloo

Point Cloates

LEGEND

Ningaloo Marine Park
Cape Range National Park
Coastal Reserve

Coral Bay • Point Maud

TROPIC OF CAPRICORN

Amherst Point

CAPE RANGE NATIONAL PARK

Cape Range National Park was originally established in 1964, with a further addition being made in 1969. It encompasses an area of 50 581 hectares comprising a large part of the limestone Cape Range and the flat coastal plain adjacent to the coast of Ningaloo Marine Park. Much of the coastal plain was formerly under pastoral lease — with the exclusion of sheep, it is slowly returning to its former state. Large numbers of red and euro kangaroos are a feature of the Park. The ranges behind are cut by spectacular gorges, and are the home of the endangered black-footed rock wallaby. At the southern end, the Yardie Creek Gorge remains flooded for the entire year, creating a unique oasis environment.

NINGALOO MARINE PARK

The Marine Park was established in May 1987. It is vested in the Western Australian National Parks and Nature Conservation Agency, and managed by the Western Australian Department of Conservation and Land Management. It spans 260 km (160 miles) of coastline from Bundegi Reef in Exmouth Gulf, around the tip of North-West Cape, and south as far as Amherst Point. It comprises

4300 km² (1720 square miles) of waters along the coast, the inshore portion being the property of the state of Western Australia, and the offshore ocean waters being the property of the Commonwealth of Australia. A strip of coastal land extending 40 m (130 ft) above High Water Mark is also included in the Park.

A management plan for the Park was published in 1989, and sanctuary zones for marine life were finally established in 1993, where particular types of marine life are to be protected. Three petroleum permits existed prior to the Park's establishment, and these areas were not included in the Commonwealth waters of the Park. Management of fisheries within the Park is controlled by federal and state Fisheries Departments.

The name 'Ningaloo Reef' was adopted because of the central location of a pastoral lease called Ningaloo Station on the coast. The word 'Ningaloo' is a local Aboriginal word meaning a point or promontory; it was the Aboriginal name of the place now known as Point Cloates.

ABOVE: Yardie Creek, at the southern end of the Cape Range National Park.

BELOW LEFT: The endangered black-footed rock wallaby thrives on the rock walls of Yardie Creek Gorge, in the foothills of the Cape Range. Its survival is currently under threat from introduced species such as foxes and feral cats.

FAR LEFT: The National Parks of the North-West Cape region.

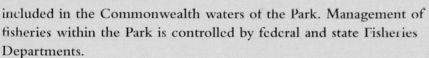

THE CORAL REEF OF NINGALOO

The contrast between the comparatively barren land environment of the Cape and the diversity of life to be found offshore, on Ningaloo Reef, could not be greater. Almost every family of tropical marine creature is represented, from minute, colourful fish to huge sailfish and marlin; from manta rays to dolphins and dugongs; and of course, a large number of various shark species.

Ningaloo Reef is unique in many ways. It stretches south from the tip of the North-West Cape for 260 km (160 miles) along the west coast of Australia. It is the only extensive coral reef in the world that occurs on the west coast of a continent. It is closer to the edge of the continental shelf than any other point of the Australian coastline.

The reef owes its existence to the Leeuwin Current; a current of warm tropical water that originates in the Pacific Ocean, flows across the north of Australia and down its west coast, maintaining the water temperature at a level suitable for coral growth.

At its southern end the reef is somewhat broken, but as you travel northwards it becomes a continuous wall of coral, pounded by the Indian Ocean swells. In some places it is only 100 m (300 ft) or so offshore; in others, it is as much as 5 km (3 miles) away, sheltering a large lagoon. Some of these lagoons support prolific coral growth, nowhere more so than at magnificent Coral Bay, south of Point Maud. Here the coral growth covers several square kilometres.

East of the North-West Cape peninsula lie the sheltered waters of Exmouth Gulf. Protected by this

FAR LEFT: *Colourful gorgonian corals are a feature of coral reefs. Their 'fans' are covered in tiny polyps, whose tentacles trap the zooplankton floating past in the water. Gorgonians are commonly found under limestone ledges.*

BELOW: *A group of inquisitive rock cod (Epinephelus species) hover over a brain coral.*

land mass from the big swells of the Indian Ocean, and subject to strong tidal currents, the northern end of the gulf supports rich coral growth and is included within the Ningaloo Marine Park. Known as Bundegi Reef, this northern end of the reef has some of the most spectacular coral growth on the coast, with many massive porites corals and prolific acropora plate corals. The eastern and southern coasts of the gulf are bordered by extensive mangrove creeks. The thick oozing mud of the mangroves is rich in nutrients and supports a unique ecosystem that is vital to the existence of the reef and its marine life.

ABOVE: *A great diversity of corals grows at Ningaloo. Here, a montipora coral competes with acropora plate corals for space, while a large porites coral grows in the background.*

BELOW: *The zones of a fringing reef.*

A Fringing Reef

Ningaloo Reef is a fringing coral reef. While the Great Barrier Reef, on the east coast of Australia, is separated from the coast by a wide expanse of deep coastal water (the distinguishing feature of a barrier reef), Ningaloo Reef follows the coast, being separated from it by a shallow lagoon. Ningaloo Reef is believed to be the longest fringing reef in the world. There are many different ecological habitats across the various zones of a fringing reef.

The ocean swells on the 'reef front' pound the outer slope of the reef with surf. Corals that grow on these outer slopes are smashed in storms, and some of the fragments are washed up onto the 'algal ridge', the ridge between the reef front and the back reef. Here, coralline algae spread out in thin layers over the coral rubble and precipitate calcium carbonate, which then cements the fragments of coral together, thus building the reef.

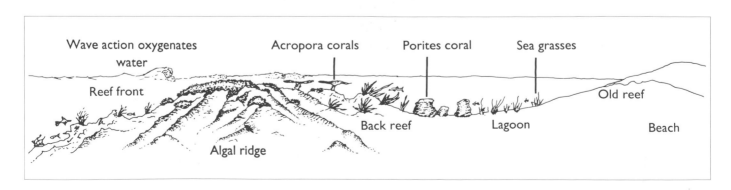

Wave action oxygenates water

Acropora corals

Porites coral

Sea grasses

Reef front

Old reef

Back reef

Lagoon

Beach

Algal ridge

Inshore from this zone is the 'reef flat' or 'back reef'. This is a zone stretching several hundred metres across where all the ingredients are right for prolific coral growth. The water is shallow, making sunlight abundant for photosynthesis. The water from the breaking surf pours over the algal ridge as a strong current, bringing with it planktonic food on which the corals feed. This water is richly oxygenated by the foaming surf. Fast-growing acropora corals grow in this zone, with plate corals and staghorns predominating. The water flows through this zone into the deeper lagoon.

The lagoon bottom is usually sandy with areas of seagrass beds that support an entirely different fauna. In areas of the lagoon where there is a solid base, stands of lagoon corals grow. The main species here are different from those of the back reef. Large porites corals form massive 'bommies', while the magnificent brain corals and faviid corals form fascinating shapes.

Further inshore, there is often a zone of shallow reef, known as the 'beach platform', before the sandy beach itself. In some areas the shoreline is old, concreted coral reef that formed at a time when the sea-level was higher.

BELOW: *Pink staghorns compete with plate corals in this stand of corals from the Acropora species. These are the principal corals to be found on the shallow back reefs of Ningaloo.*

THE NUTRIENT WEB OF CORAL REEFS

There is one thing common to all creatures on earth. In order to live and to grow, they need basic nutrients. The basic nutrients required for energy are different from those required for growth.

For energy, sugars and carbohydrates are required. These are created by plants in the process known as photosynthesis: using energy from the sun, plants are able to combine water and carbon dioxide into sugars.

In order to grow, plants and animals need to make proteins from the basic building blocks — amino acids. Amino acids are made by plants and require basic elements, the most important of which are nitrogen and phosphorus.

The enigma of coral reefs is that they exist in oceans that have very low concentrations of these basic elements, nitrogen and phosphorus. (Nitrogen and phosphorus are present in the oceans as nitrates, nitrites, salts, ammonium and phosphate.) Corals are animals, but many have evolved a unique and interdependent relationship with an algae (plants that

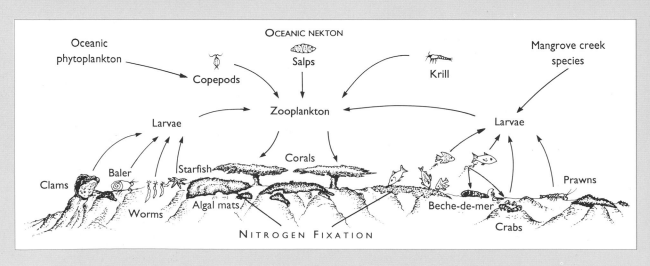

are known as zooanthellae) that lives within their cells. (Such corals are known as hermatypic corals.) These zooanthellae are able to photosynthesise, providing the coral polyp with sugars and energy. The coral polyps still need protein, however, in order to grow, and they obtain this by feeding on the zooplankton that are washed over the reef.

These zooplankton, brought to the reef by the ocean currents, are the key to the survival of coral reefs. They come from different environments. Some, such as the copepods, graze on the plant plankton — the phytoplankton — of the open ocean. Others are the larvae of creatures that live on the reef itself, and still others are the larvae of creatures that live in the creeks and mangroves along the coastline.

ABOVE: Melithea squamata, *a gorgonian, or sea fan, growing with stinging 'feathery' hydroids on the coral at Bundegi Reef.*

FAR TOP LEFT: *Red squirrelfish hide in holes in the limestone under a ledge.*

FAR BOTTOM LEFT: *The nitrogen food web of a coral reef.*

The Growth of the Coral Reef

The growth and formation of coral reefs is one of the wonders of the natural world, and for many years scientists have puzzled over the paradox that they represent. The clear, warm waters of tropical regions are relatively devoid of the important dissolved nutrients, nitrogen and phosphate, essential to the growth of marine organisms, and the traditional view of marine biologists regarding tropical waters is that they are marine 'deserts'. And yet the coral reefs are oases of productivity. How the reefs are able to extract sufficient nutrients from the surrounding ocean to sustain themselves has been the subject of much study. The greatest mystery of all is how the coral obtains sufficient nitrogen from its nutrient-poor environment in order to make protein and grow. Essential to every food chain are creatures that are able to 'fix' nitrogen, incorporating it into more complex molecules and making it available for other organisms to use for growth.

It turns out that the reefs are complex ecosystems where every creature has a role to play in the web of the food chain.

Many coral species derive their energy (for which they need carbohydrates or sugars) from a remarkable symbiotic relationship with an algae that lives in their outer gastro-dermal layer. These algae, known as zooanthellae, are a type of dinoflagellate that live within the cells of the coral polyp and are able to photosynthesise, harnessing the sun's energy to produce carbohydrates (sugars) that feed the coral polyp. The zooanthellae profit by this relationship as the coral polyp in turn provides them with a stable, protected environment and with protein. This type of symbiotic relationship is common in the marine environment; there are many other invertebrate species with a similar association. Its discovery was a major breakthrough in understanding how corals obtain energy. However, this relationship does not explain the phenomenal growth of coral.

To grow, corals need proteins. The coral polyps are carnivorous, obtaining protein from the plankton that they catch in the water. Their tentacles are covered in stinger cells, 'nematocysts', which are used to inject their prey with poison. The tentacles then move the food down to the mouth for ingestion.

The coral polyp bridges the gap between the plant world and the animal world, deriving its food

BELOW: *Anatomy of a coral polyp.*

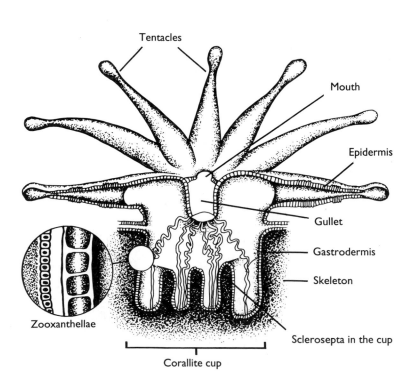

Tentacles

Mouth

Epidermis

Gullet

Gastrodermis

Skeleton

Zooxanthellae

Sclerosepta in the cup

Corallite cup

both from photosynthesis and from protein-consumption, enjoying the best of both worlds.

Living in an ocean that has few nutrients, it is vital that the reef keep protein within the reef system. It is thought that much of the plankton consumed by the coral is the larval stage of creatures that live on the reef as adults.

Plankton are organisms that live in the open parts of the ocean, whose movements are thus largely determined by the ocean currents. There are two types of plankton: zooplankton are animals, herbivores or carnivores; phytoplankton are photosynthesising plants. Many zooplankton organisms spend only a part of their life cycle as plankton. These organisms are known as the meroplankton, and many of them are the tiny larvae of creatures that live on the reef itself — crabs, crayfish, shrimps and prawns. Other creatures, the holoplankton, remain planktonic for their whole lives. The commonest zooplankton, copepods, are herbivorous, grazing on the phytoplankton. They themselves are the food of larger carnivorous zooplankton, such as krill. All these organisms are to be found in the plankton at Ningaloo Reef. While moving through the oceans at the whim of ocean currents, many of the zooplankton are able to travel large vertical distances. They hide in the depths during the day and migrate to the surface at night.

This explains why, when you dive on many coral reefs of the world during the day, the waters are crystal clear, with no sign of the food that might nourish the reef. To complete the picture of a coral reef, you have to dive at night. During the day, with the plankton hiding on the ocean floor, the corals rest, their tentacles withdrawn. At night, waters that were previously clear become thick with these planktonic organisms that have migrated toward the surface. This is when the corals open their tentacles to feed in earnest — the reef at night has been described as a 'wall of mouths'. As the ocean swells break over the reef platform, the combined tentacles of the corals are like a huge sieve, capturing the plankton that is carried across the reef and that provides the protein, and the nitrogen, for the reef to continue to grow.

Tropical oceans have very low concentrations of essential phosphate and nitrogen. Creatures that are able to 'fix' nitrogen in this environment and make it available to the rest of the food chain are crucial to maintaining the growth of the reef. It has been shown that the encrusting blue-green algaes that coat the

ABOVE: *Mantis shrimp stomatopod larvae and megalopa-stage crab decapod larvae — these are portunid crabs. Stomatopods and decapods have been found together in abundance on the ocean floor of Exmouth Gulf. It seems likely that they originate there.*

reef top and live on exposed reefs are able to fulfil this role, fixing dissolved nitrogen and making it available as organic molecules to the rest of the food chain. Other creatures graze on the algae, resulting in the protein entering the food chain. The parrotfish and surgeonfish, for example, patrol the reef, continually grazing on the algal mats, thus playing a vital role. Much of the nitrogenous material is passed by the fish as faeces, which is itself ingested by other organisms, whose larvae become part of the plankton. Hence, the drab-looking algaes of the reef flats play a very important role in providing nutrients for the reef.

The import of protein (in the form of plankton) into the reef from other sources will determine the ability of the reef to grow and to recover from damage. Coral reefs are damaged all the time by a number of natural processes, from fish feeding on the coral to tropical cyclones, as well as by human influences. Ningaloo Reef exists only because of a very special ocean current: the warm Leeuwin Current, which originates in the Pacific Ocean and brings warm tropical water sweeping across the north of Australia and down the west coast of the continent. It maintains the water temperature at a level suitable for coral growth. It may also play another important role.

North of North-West Cape, the Western Australian coast is made up largely of mangrove creeks. For many people, the mosquito-ridden stands of mangroves are thought of as an inhospitable, impenetrable place, but they play an important role in the food chains of tropical waters. The rich mud of mangrove creeks is an organic soup, full of bacteria and fungi that are able to fix nitrogen. There is even one family of mangrove, Lumnitzera, that has bacteria in its leaves that can fix nitrogen. As a result, the mangrove communities are highly productive and the home of large numbers of crustaceans, molluscs and fish. When these creatures spawn, their larvae enter the oceanic plankton to form a large proportion of the zooplankton that is to be found in the tropical waters of the region.

Ningaloo Reef may also owe its existence to the large amount of nutrients in the form of zooplankton

BELOW: *Mangroves are a rich source of nitrogen for tropical oceans. It appears likely that the huge mangrove systems to the north-east of Ningaloo Reef play an important role in maintaining the reef.*

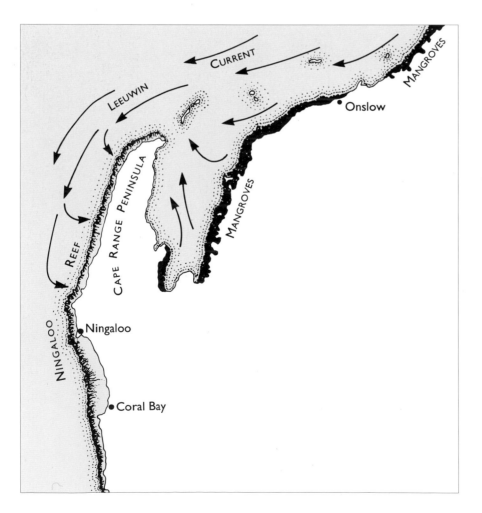

brought down by the Leeuwin Current from these massive mangrove systems to the north. Indeed, for many years, fishermen at Exmouth have maintained that Exmouth Gulf is the nursery for the whole reef. They were referring to fish, but in a broader sense, their instinctive ideas may not be far from the truth, given that the southern and eastern coastlines of the Gulf both have extensive mangrove systems.

When we look at a stand of coral on a coral reef, it is easy to think that it is unchanging — after all, corals have hard, bony-looking skeletons made of calcium carbonate. The truth is very different: the reef is extremely dynamic, changing from season to season, and also extremely vulnerable. Some species of corals, such as the acroporas, are fast-growing, up to 20 cm (8 in) per year. They are continually competing with neighbouring corals for space on the reef. In the shallow waters where coral growth is most prolific, a stand of coral may be smashed to pieces one year by a winter storm or a tropical cyclone and the surviving polyps will regenerate in a few years. Meanwhile, the damaged coral falls to the bottom as rubble, which is then concreted together by coralline algae and becomes part of the solid platform of the reef itself.

ABOVE: *The brightly coloured coral Turbinara reniformis can be found from the tropics to temperate waters. It is ahermatypic (without zooanthellae), relying wholly on zooplankton for its sustenance.*

FISH OF THE REEF

Coral reefs are famous for their fish and Ningaloo Reef is no exception. A huge variety of fish live among the corals, and each family occupies a unique ecological niche. Some fish, like the beautiful angelfish, graze on the coral itself, sucking the polyps out of the limestone skeleton. The large, colourful parrotfish species have powerful beaks, and crunch into the coral, consuming it limestone and all. The solid limestone is not absorbed, but passes through them and is excreted. They are largely responsible for the production of the fine coral sands of the beaches.

Within coral colonies hide many species of colourful damselfish. They shelter in the coral for protection, feeding on algae and plankton brought by the currents, and will vigorously defend their chosen home from attack by the grazing parrotfish.

Other fish are herbivorous and live on the algae that grow beneath and between the corals. A common sight at Ningaloo Reef is a mixed school of striped surgeonfish and small parrotfish cruising the reef, feeding voraciously on the algae. These fish are extremely important to the reef, as without them,

BELOW: *A brown sweetlip,* Plectorhinchus gibbosus, *hides under a curtain of cardinalfish at a reef feeding station.*

the corals would be overwhelmed by algae. They also play a vital role as they release the nitrogen produced by the algae into the food chain.

Also hiding in and under the corals are the larger predatory fish that feed on the juvenile, the infirm and the careless fish of the reef, thus maintaining the balance of the reef ecosystem. Each fish family has a role to play in the reef's stability.

As well as its permanent residents, the reef environment also attracts visiting fish to the area. Pelagic fish (fish that live in the open ocean) that migrate along the coast come to feed, and some species also spawn there. The Spanish mackerel is one such species. It arrives on the reef front in large numbers during the winter months, providing some exciting game-fishing opportunities. This species grows to a length of up to 2.3 m (7½ ft). Other species, such as wahoo, mahi mahi, queenfish and numerous species of trevally, or jacks, provide variety for the angler. The greatest fishing 'trophies' are the billfish — Ningaloo Reef can boast all three species of marlin found in Australian waters, the black, blue and striped marlins, as well as the sailfish. Thankfully, anglers are now tagging and releasing most of these magnificent creatures, so that sailfish are still abundant at Ningaloo Reef.

ABOVE LEFT: *The magnificent coral cod,* Cephalopholis miniata.

ABOVE RIGHT: *A school of two surgeonfish species — yellow convict tangs,* Acanthurus triostegus *(foreground), and bristle-toothed surgeonfish,* Ctenochaetus strigosus.

BELOW: *A parrotfish, of the Scaridae species, sleeps in its cocoon of mucus, hidden in the coral at night. Parrotfish graze on the algae and corals nearby.*

TURTLE-HATCHING SEASON

There are many exciting features of the marine life at Ningaloo, with each season bringing a different wildlife spectacle. Every year in December, with the approach of summer, a strange phenomenon is encountered — rafts of turtles. Green turtles mostly, along with loggerhead and hawksbill turtles, return to the area to breed, congregating in the lagoon and particularly off the northern beaches of the Cape. The male turtles pursue the females and mount them in the open sea. As one couple mates, a ring of eager males gathers round, each waiting its turn. The exhausted females eventually seek refuge by crawling up to the beaches.

Soon the female turtles can be found coming up onto the northern beaches at night to lay their eggs. They start by digging a pit with their front flippers until they reach firm sand, then they use their back flippers to dig down vertically, constructing the egg chamber. They then deposit between 90 and 100 eggs in the hole. However, their work is by no means finished. They fill in the hole, then spend several hours digging forward with their front flippers, flicking the sand behind them as they go. The hollow that they eventually leave is several metres away from the nest site, which is thus 'disguised'. Research has shown that the temperature of the nest will determine the sex of the turtles that hatch.

The baby turtles hatch out of their eggs between January and March, and must fight their way up through the sand to the surface. They then have to run the gauntlet of marauding crabs and seagulls to make the water's edge. As they swim out to sea, they are also easy prey for fish. And if they make it, they become yet another of Ningaloo's unsolved mysteries: nobody knows where the young turtles go, or where they spend their early years. They are not seen again until many years later, when some 'adolescent' turtles return to the coast to live in the mangrove creeks, fossicking among the roots and grazing on the algae.

BELOW: *A female green turtle retreats to the beach to rest, and to escape the attentions of the males.*

THE REEF SPAWNS

It is March, and the turtles have almost finished their laying season. As the sun hits the horizon in the west, the full moon rises out of the waters of the Exmouth Gulf. Offshore on the reef, changes are occurring. Inside the cells of hundreds of different species, gametes are maturing in preparation for one of nature's most fascinating occurrences. Seven days after the full moon, one hour after dark, the reef spawns.

It is incredible that this amazing phenomenon was unknown to scientists until the early 1980s, when it was discovered on the Great Barrier Reef, off the east coast of Australia. We now know that not only are the corals spawning in this incredible orgy, but so are species of polychaete worms, seaslugs, molluscs and possibly many others. The coral polyps release their eggs and semen in bundles, which can be seen with the naked eye. They float up to the surface and are carried away by the currents. In areas of heavy spawning, the spawn forms slicks. After a while the bundles swell and rupture, releasing their contents. Fertilisation takes place and a living planktonic animal is born — the coral planula. This creature may spend several weeks floating in the ocean as part of the plankton before eventually swimming to the sea floor in search of a suitably hard substrate upon which to settle and then grow into a new coral. It is amazing that the timing of this phenomenon is related to the phases of the moon. On the Barrier Reef it occurs every year in spring, after the October and November full moons.

It was not until March 1984 that biologist Chris Simpson, who was working in the Dampier Archipelago off Western Australia, discovered that this same spawning phenomenon also occurs on the west coast of Australia, at a completely different time of year — every autumn (fall). We now know that on the Western Australian coast, spawning happens after the March and April full moons each year, usually on the seventh to the ninth night after the full moon. There are other species that spawn simultaneously with the coral, also releasing a massive load of protein into the waters of the reef. Overnight, waters that are normally depleted of protein become a rich bouillabaisse of nutrients.

BELOW: *A coral spawns soon after dusk, releasing egg and sperm bundles, which float slowly to the surface.*

ABOVE: *In the sheltered waters of Coral Bay, large slicks of spawn can be seen the morning after a heavy spawning, the result of millions of tiny, bright pink egg and sperm bundles bursting from the coral polyps and floating to the surface.*

This huge protein release has far-reaching effects for the whole region. Tidal and ocean currents are responsible for disseminating the spawn. The Leeuwin Current takes the spawn south — it is claimed that the spawning on Ningaloo Reef and Bundegi Reef plays a role in sustaining the corals of the Abrolhos Archipelago, which is over 700 km (440 miles) further south. However, if this strong current removed all the spawn from the ecosystem, the loss of protein to the reef itself would be devastating. Thankfully, this does not occur. Our studies at Ningaloo have shown that throughout March and early April, a current flows north along the reef front, acting as a countercurrent to the Leeuwin Current, which flows further offshore. At the southern end of the reef the Leeuwin Current throws off a large eddy that brings the planktonic stream back in to the reef front, where it circulates north again. Thus, the huge amount of protein released in the reef's annual reproductive effort remains largely within the reef system.

THE ANNUAL FEEDING FRENZY

In the weeks following the reef spawning, the zooplankton food chain takes off. One dramatic discovery at Ningaloo has been the swarms of the tropical krill *Pseudeuphausia latifrons* that spawn at this time and travel north along the reef front. They are only 8–10 mm (¼–⅓ in) in length, and are a favourite food of whale sharks. Like other zooplankton, they move vertically in the water, and usually only rise to the surface at night. An exception to this is during spawning, when you can see huge swarms in the daytime at Ningaloo, laden with eggs.

The swarms attract the plankton feeders. This is the only time of year when it is possible to see whale sharks feeding during the daytime, and it may only last for one or two days. Large numbers of sharks rise to the surface with mouths agape and charge through the swarms of krill, thrashing their tails from side to side. Mobulid rays and manta rays also appear and, using the ocean swells, they charge down the wave fronts, flapping their 'wings', and crash through the krill. But it is the sight of a group of huge whale sharks charging back and forth in a feeding frenzy that is arguably the most exciting.

The bloom of zooplankton also provides food for small fish. On a calm day in April the surface of the sea off the reef is full of tiny fish. Every piece of seaweed is used for shelter. Where the fish come from is not known, but they are probably juveniles of reef-dwelling species that have spawned at this time of year to give their offspring the best chance of survival. Schools of anchovies appear along the reef and themselves attract pelagic predators — schools of tuna and trevally species. The predators round up the anchovies into tight fishballs on the surface, and this attracts birds such as the wedge-tailed shearwaters, which dive down into the water to snatch fish from the fishball. All this excitement attracts the predatory sharks, and black-tip reef sharks and bronze whalers come to join the feast.

This glut of food attracts the largest predators of all — the rorqual whales. We now know that the particular type of rorqual whales visiting Ningaloo are Brydes whales. They attack the fishballs from below, rolling on their sides with mouths wide open, consuming hundreds of fish with each mouthful.

In May, as the winter approaches in the southern hemisphere, larger planktonic creatures appear. Huge numbers of opaque gelatinous creatures arrive together. They occupy the same ecological niche but they are not all 'jellyfish' — in the world of jellyfish, appearances can be deceptive. Many of these creatures that have evolved similar appearances are from very different branches of the animal kingdom.

Some of them, like the harmless common button jellyfish *Aurelia*, are true jellyfish, belonging to the phylum Cnidaria. Some members of this phylum are powerful stingers, such as the *Pelagia* genus, which may attack

BELOW: *A chain of salps, part of the zooplankton. These vertebrates nurse their young, which can be seen inside the adult salps.*

BOTTOM: *A sample of the krill, Pseudeuphausia latifrons, collected 8 m (26 ft) below the surface while diving at night outside the reef. This tropical species of krill grows to 10 mm (⅓ in) and is a favourite food of the whale sharks.*

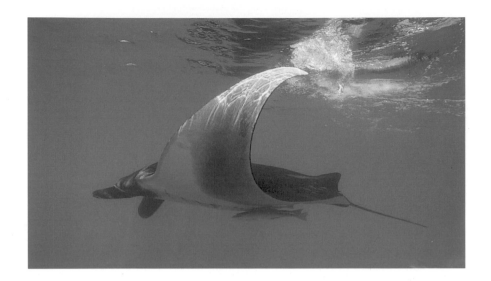

other jellyfish, including the *Aurelia*. The Cnidaria are more closely related to the corals than to the Ctenophora, or comb jellies, which look so like them. These have rows of cilia (short, hair-like extensions of cells) that beat rapidly, moving the creature around and filtering out tiny plankton. Some comb jellies found at Ningaloo Reef also have a pair of stinging tentacles. Then there are the Pteropoda, members of the mollusc family that have no shell. Some of them resemble gelatinous butterflies. Lastly, there are the salps, which belong to the phylum Chordata, subphylum Tunicata. These remarkable creatures are related to the ascidians, or sea squirts, and are like a mobile sea squirt. They develop from eggs that are joined together in long chains, and they remain attached as colonies. Huge numbers of these salps appear along the reef front in the months following the reef spawning.

As the winter progresses, the larger predatory fish appear on the reef front to feed on the smaller fish that have congregated to feed on the zooplankton. Spanish mackerel, queenfish, wahoo, tuna and trevally species feed on the mullet and garfish that are feeding lower down the food chain. By August, large numbers of sailfish are also schooling on the reef.

The zooplankton bloom continues, and throughout July, large numbers of manta rays can be found feeding in areas thick with plankton. The manta ray grows so large that it has been feared by anglers for many generations, and in the past was given the name 'devil ray', probably because when it rolls up the fins on its head, they look like horns. The rays swim in lines, up to 50 in a row, back and forth along the reef front at this time of year.

ABOVE: *A giant manta ray, Manta birostris. Large schools can be found swimming along the reef during mid-winter, feeding on the zooplankton.*

BELOW LEFT: *Salps are unique gelatinous zooplankton that have many of the features of vertebrates.*

BELOW RIGHT: *The larva of the mantis shrimp stomatopod.*

MIGRATION OF THE HUMPBACK WHALES

At the same time, some of the largest filter feeders in the world are arriving. The humpback whales pass along Ningaloo Reef on their northern migration, with the first pods arriving in late June. How far north they go is still not known, but many of them continue on past Broome. Earlier this century, large numbers of humpback whales were slaughtered by the whaling vessels based at the Norwegian Bay whaling station at Ningaloo. Records from the whaling station show that in the 1950s, the quota was 600 whales per year, and on a good day (a day of fine weather) up to 15 humpback whales would be slaughtered. Three whale chasers operated from the station at this time. The wreck of one whale chaser, *Fin*, which was washed onto the reef in 1923, can still be seen close to Fraser Island. The whaling station is now a tangled mass of rusting iron.

The question is often asked: do the whales feed during their migration? Those whales slaughtered at Norwegian Bay had empty stomachs, so it appears that they visit the warm tropical waters for one purpose only, to procreate. Further north, beyond Ningaloo, the pregnant females will give birth, while the other mature females will spend a lot of the season being followed around by bull whales eager to mate. The whales continue their northward migration until mid-September. Some of the earlier groups are by then already beginning to return south. The southward migration is far more protracted than the one northward. Mothers accompanied by their calves spend several weeks in the sheltered bays of Exmouth Gulf and Shark Bay.

BELOW: *A sub-adult humpback whale breeches off North-West Cape. The pleated flesh of the throat allows this whale to take in huge quantities of water when it feeds.*

ABOVE: *A humpback whale thrashes its tail down on the surface of the water repeatedly — this is known as 'tail-lobbing'. The markings of a humpback whale's tail are like a fingerprint, allowing individual whales to be identified.*

In the early part of winter, around June and July, the waters of these bays cool to below 20°C (68°F), but after August they warm up again and the humpback whales enjoy the 25°–26°C (77°–79°F) water temperature. The largest numbers of whales pass through the area in October, and the last of them do not leave the area until the end of December.

OTHER RESIDENTS OF THE REEF

The Ningaloo Marine Park is home to other cetaceans. Bottle-nosed dolphins are often seen in small family groups cruising in the lagoons. In recent years the shy Indo–Pacific humpback dolphin has also become common. In April 1992 a huge school of spinner dolphins was sighted offshore. These dolphins are so named because of their habit of spinning around as they leap from the water — a spectacular sight.

Killer whales are infrequent visitors to Ningaloo. More common are large schools of false killer whales, which charge down the reef front pursuing their prey. On one occasion a 2-m (6-ft) sailfish was seen tail-walking across the ocean pursued by a school of these whales. Another occasional visitor is the pygmy killer whale. Travelling in large schools, these whales leap clear of the water when in pursuit of schools of fish.

There is one marine mammal living in these sheltered waters that is the source of many myths and legends. The dugong, or sea cow, is thought to be the origin of the mermaid legends. A herbivore, grazing on sea grasses, it is rarely seen because of its elusive nature. It is now considered an endangered species because of the destruction of large numbers of the animal throughout much of its habitat range in South-East Asia. However, aerial surveys of tropical Australian waters suggest that it is the commonest marine mammal in the northern waters of Australia, existing in greater numbers than dolphins. It lives mainly in the sheltered areas of the gulfs and bays of northern Australia. As the enclosed waters of Exmouth Gulf cool in May, June and July, large numbers of dugong migrate around the Cape to the warmer Indian Ocean waters of the west coast. Here they can be found moving along the reef and feeding on the sea-grass beds of the lagoon. The dugong has one calf every three years, and the calves remain with their mothers until the next offspring is born. This low rate of fecundity is a major concern for the species' survival.

THE CYCLE CONTINUES

As the last humpback whales are leaving Exmouth Gulf in December, the turtles are once again starting their struggle up the beaches of North-West Cape. The Ningaloo year has come full circle.

BELOW: *A pregnant dugong (underneath), or sea cow, cruises with her mature calf.*

NINGALOO REEF IN ART

The diverse marine life and extraordinary natural beauty of Ningaloo Reef have inspired a number of Australian artists. Using their preferred medium, they have all interpreted the reef in their own way.

Artist Ian Dickinson trained and worked as a graphic artist in the eastern states of Australia before moving to the west coast. He lives with his wife, Sue, at the Milyering Visitor Centre in the Cape Range National Park, on the western side of the North-West Cape. From his house, Ian looks out over the sand-dunes and the turquoise waters of the lagoon. On still mornings, the thundering of the surf on the reef can be heard.

In this isolated setting Ian has explored the underwater world, using a meticulous style to reveal the fine detail of the reef. He started painting small, detailed pictures of individual animals, and now produces large, composite images that show the diversity and profusion of colour of the fish and corals on the reef. Some of his most impressive recent paintings have been of whale sharks cruising through the azure-blue ocean over the coral outcrops vibrant with marine life.

Leon Pericles has been described as one of the *enfants terribles* of the Australian art scene. As an art teacher in his younger days, he was reputed to dress in the style of the art he intended to teach that day. His work displays a unique and rare talent; he is able to translate his roguish sense of humour into his work.

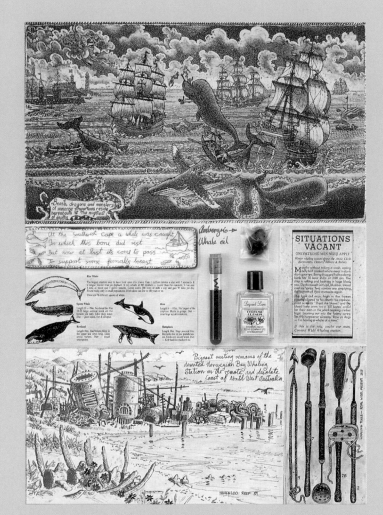

Leon has visited the Ningaloo area several times, and in 1989 he was invited to be artist-in-residence at the Milyering Visitor Centre. He works in a variety of mediums, but is best known for his lithographs, which are produced using the traditional methods of the great lithographers of the Middle Ages. With this medium, Leon produces images that have a satirical edge and often, at the same time, an educative intent.

Wendy Lugg describes herself as a fibre artist and quilt maker. Trained as an artist, she has a fascination with textiles, and now concentrates on producing large wall-hangings. She combines a number of techniques, including fabric printing and patchwork quilting, to exploit the different textures and colours of her materials, creating vibrant works that transcend mere craft. She has been invited to exhibit her work in Japan and the United States, and has won awards in the United Kingdom. Her marine images, inspired by Ningaloo Reef, are alive with the colours of the ocean.

Joanna Taylor, my wife, has similarly explored the use of rich fabric colours to create quilts that capture the mood of the sea and the diversity of the creatures to be found at Ningaloo Reef. Joanna has accompanied me on many expeditions to search for whale sharks, humpback whales, manta rays, turtles and dugongs, and all these marine creatures feature in her brilliantly coloured quilts.

The work of these artists is featured on these pages. It may give those who have never visited Ningaloo Reef a sense of the excitement and beauty of this most remarkable place.

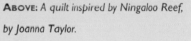

ABOVE: *A quilt inspired by Ningaloo Reef, by Joanna Taylor.*

LEFT: Reef, *wall-hanging by Wendy Lugg.*

OPPOSITE TOP: Leviathan Lament, *etching by Leon Pericles, 1989.*

OPPOSITE BOTTOM: Whale Sharks over the Reef, *painting by Ian Dickinson.*

CHAPTER 5

A PERSONAL ADVENTURE

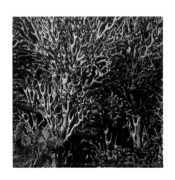

For the last twelve years of my life, the whale shark has been something of an obsession. What began as a desire to see a whale shark in its natural habitat and to dive with it, soon turned into a personal quest to photograph and to closely study these rare creatures, in order to gain a deeper understanding of them and their marine environment.

GETTING HOOKED ON WHALE SHARKS

The story of my involvement with the whale shark really began in 1980. After arriving in Western Australia in the late 1970s, my wife Joanna and I had become keen divers. In May 1980 we joined a team of divers from the Western Australian Maritime Museum on the remote west coast, at Ningaloo Station. We were diving on the wreck of a ship that went down in 1811 at Point Cloates. The identity of the wreck was unknown, but expedition leader Graeme Henderson later discovered that it was the *Rapid*, which had sailed from Boston, in the United States.

Joanna and I, as relative newcomers to Western Australia and also as novice divers, were unaware that in that remote spot there was assembled a 'who's who' of Western Australian diving. The Western Australian Museum is respected throughout the world for its expertise in wreck excavation. The team was led by Graeme Henderson and supported by Mike McCarthy and Jeff Kimpton. Pat Baker and Brian Richards were there for photography, while in the conservation department, there were 'Professor' Ian MacLeod, James Pang and Moira Stanbury. Among the volunteers assembled were author Hugh Edwards, Dr Johnny Williams from Augusta; the Paxman brothers, who had discovered the wreck, and the Stagg brothers, who had also searched for it. The organisation was incredible. Some were lucky enough to camp in the shearers' quarters of the sheep station; the rest of us rolled out our swags in the sheep pens. Everyone helped with the catering.

We were there courtesy of Edgar and Billie Lefroy, the owners of Ningaloo Station. Edgar had lived in this remote spot since the Second World War, and was a fascinating character with many a good yarn. Both Edgar and Billie were to become friends and patients of mine when I moved my medical practice to Exmouth in 1982. Sadly, Edgar died of cancer in 1987, taking with him a wealth of local knowledge.

It was a memorable holiday, living in the station shearing shed, and diving and excavating the wreck. Strolling along the white coral sand beaches with the surf pounding the reef offshore and glistening in the tropical sun, we fell in love with this magnificent coast. In the afternoons we were free to go exploring — to the reefs offshore, or to Fraser Island, where the whale chaser *Fin* is wrecked, or the old whaling station at Norwegian Bay, or up to the old lighthouse that adorns the huge sandhills of Point Cloates. All these places have a remarkable history.

One afternoon there was great excitement in the camp. A team of divers had been searching for the wreck of a Japanese warship. On their way home they had sighted a whale shark. Museum diver Jeff Kimpton had snorkelled with the shark, then been towed along on its dorsal fin. They returned to the camp full of tales of their experience. A whale shark at Ningaloo! I decided then and there that if I got a chance to return to this remote coast, I would search out one of these huge yet elusive creatures.

PREVIOUS PAGE: *The April sunrise over the sand dunes of Ningaloo, to the south of Point Cloates.*

ON THE TRAIL OF THE WHALE SHARK

It was two years before Joanna and I were to return to Ningaloo Reef. Tiring of the 'rat race' of city life and large hospitals in Perth, I had decided to start practising as a country general practitioner — for me, it had always seemed one of the greatest challenges of medicine. The country doctor has to cope with the whole spectrum of medicine, from trivial problems to major emergencies. There is no greater test of medical resourcefulness. Where better to practise than the small town of Exmouth? Lying at the northern end of the North-West Cape, the town largely owes its existence to the huge Naval Communications Station (a joint Australian–United States facility). It is also the gateway to the northern end of Ningaloo Reef.

Little did I know in 1982 that Exmouth was to become my home for the next 11 years. There were many challenges and obstacles to be overcome. First there was the attitude of the local population. Any doctor who left the city,

ABOVE: Ningaloo Station, the pastoral station — the shearing sheds are close to the beach, the airstrip behind them. Norwegian Bay is in the background.

ABOVE: *The Indian Ocean swells break over the reef and roll on into the coral lagoon, bringing life into this fragile ecosystem. The surf oxygenates the water and carries nutrients in the form of plankton to the corals of the reef.*

it seemed, was probably 'no good'. In the first weeks I was inundated with requests for referrals to specialists in Perth. Having solved their problems, at least my patients knew that I wasn't going to be a source of free plane tickets to Perth on the government-sponsored travel scheme. There were still others who remained concerned and suspicious of a doctor who had given up specialist training to move to the bush — not least among them were my own family. There had been an expectation, because of my academic background, that I would follow the accepted route of a medical career to a specialist post back in England. But I had decided to follow a less well-travelled road.

On my weekends off, Joanna and I spent long hours exploring Ningaloo Reef in our 5-m (17-ft) motor cruiser. In the waters around the Cape we soon discovered the enormous richness and abundance of the marine life. A few months before our journey north, I had purchased a small 8-mm cinecamera, and I was keen to capture on film all the wonderful creatures of the reef. Almost every type of marine life that one might hope to find in tropical waters could be found there.

Our first sortie, on 1 May 1982, was a memorable one, with barely a ripple on the water and no swell at all. American Ted Smyer and his wife Tish had offered to show us the west coast. With our two-week-old daughter, Julia, asleep in her bassinette in the cabin, we motored north outside the reef with mackerel lines astern. At the northern end of the reef, we were astonished to find two small whale sharks basking on the surface in the calm waters. Ted had seen whale sharks before and was sure of their identity, but Joanna was less certain. Because of my new responsibilities as a father, I was quickly instructed that this was not a safe place to go diving. It was almost exactly two years since the Ningaloo whale shark sighting by the museum divers.

Not that Joanna's fears were entirely groundless. Later the same day we all stopped to snorkel on some shallow reef further north. We were in about 4 m (13 ft) of water. All of a sudden I noticed a huge shape cruising towards us along the bottom. Its tail stopped moving and it glided in towards me to lie motionless on the bottom below. This was no whale shark — it was 3.5 m (12 ft) long and slate-grey in colour; with its broad head, it could only be a tiger shark. The seconds ticked by, and then, with a flick of its powerful tail, it accelerated past beneath us and disappeared.

At that time in Exmouth it was hard to find divers who were willing to dive outside the reef along the west coast. Game-fishermen told many stories of the huge sharks to be found out there. However, I was lucky to find a dive buddy who was willing to try just about anything … once. Peter Moore was an experienced diver who had dived in New Guinea and was used to encounters with sharks.

One dive with Peter was particularly memorable for a shark encounter. The North-West Reef, on the northern tip of the Cape, is both exposed and dangerous, with strong tidal currents. It comes up sheer from the depths off the North-West Cape. We were determined to dive there. Large potato cod and schools of pelagic fish were common. We had only been down for a short time when a 2-m (6-ft) grey whaler shark started circling us, keeping his distance. Peter decided to wave at the shark: 'Hi there'. It turned in an instant and charged straight at us. The offending arm was rapidly withdrawn and the shark veered away at the last moment, only a few feet from us. Peter doesn't wave at sharks any more.

BELOW: *Joanna, my wife, emerging from a cave. The reef is covered in golden cardinalfish.*

ABOVE: *Filming a whale shark. To capture the size of this creature, and the excitement of the experience of diving with it, can be a difficult task.*

PERSEVERANCE PAYS OFF

Throughout the winter months of 1982, accompanied by friends and family, I searched along the west coast almost every fortnight for the whale sharks, but in vain. We enjoyed some great scuba-diving and learned much about the reef and about game-fishing, but I was determined to once again find the sharks. The summer sea-breezes brought rough seas from which we often retreated, and with March and the approach of autumn, I looked forward to calmer weather.

Peter and I made our plans. We tried to avoid alarming our wives with our intentions of diving with and filming the whale sharks, and jokingly referred to them as 'Woolworths supermarkets', while tiger sharks were known as 'Target supermarkets'.

At last, on 14 March, we succeeded. We found some whale sharks and managed to dive with and film them (see page 16). In all, we dived with three whale sharks that day, and spotted another two as the boat motored home along the reef. Two weeks later we dived with a further seven sharks, and I managed to get several minutes of Super-8 film footage. Twelve sightings, over a two-week period, of one of the rarest creatures in the world — something very special seemed to be happening.

MORE PLANS, MORE FRUSTRATIONS, MORE PAY-OFFS

The west coast of the Cape is no place for the faint-hearted. In March and April of that year there were very few tourists in the north, and there were many days when my boat was the only one on the water along the entire west coast — self-sufficiency and boating proficiency were essential.

With this in mind, in 1984 I decided to buy a larger boat, one that would allow me to operate more safely down the west coast. It needed to be stable enough to put an observation gantry on the roof for spotting the sharks. Joanna and I searched in Perth for ten days and fell in love with a 7-m (23-ft) Baron sitting in the boatyard of Court Yachts, a business owned by the Courts, the well-known political family in Western Australia. It was the first boat to come out of the new Baron 'Sea-Eagle' mould, and did she fly! With twin 125 hp Volvo inboard–outboard motors, she had the power to get out of sticky situations and the stability to be equipped with an observation gantry. Unfortunately, the boat-trailer needed a lot of work before we could contemplate the 1200-km (720-mile) trip back up to Exmouth. Our departure was delayed several times, but we eventually made the journey, driving all through the night, to arrive with only three days left before I had to return to work. It was 14 April and the weather was great — there had to be whale sharks out there.

Joanna and I searched up and down the northern end of the reef in the new boat for those three days, full of expectation, but we saw no sign of a whale shark. We took the boat out again on the following weekends, but within two weeks it was blowing a gale and we were unable to continue the search. It looked as if we had missed the whole season.

However, with the new boat, I was able to explore the west coast even in rough weather. In July I took Wes Dean, a pilot with the Flying Doctor Service, fishing outside the reef. We were anchored about 500 m (1600 ft) offshore from the reef when a whale shark swam up to the back of the boat and stayed there for several minutes. It seemed to be as intrigued with us as we were with it, and I had time to unpack the cinecamera and take some footage.

BELOW: *The first encounter with a mouth as big and as wide as this one can be a heart-stopping experience.*

My next encounter was while game-fishing in January 1985. We were competing in a club competition over the Australia Day long weekend. It was a sensational day, with us hooking several sailfish. As the first sailfish took the bait and started tail-walking across the water only 20 m (65 ft) behind the boat, a huge whale shark surfaced right behind the transom and swam through all the remaining lines, which we were desperately trying to retrieve. Later the same day we made another sighting.

I telephoned friends in Perth to tell them the news: the whale sharks were here already. If they came north to Ningaloo in early March for a holiday, I felt confident we would see more.

The holiday was organised for the first week of March. For the whole week we braved the strong sea-breezes and rough seas, and only had a brief sighting of one whale shark. Our friends departed, bitterly disappointed.

Then over the Easter long weekend in April, there were whale sharks everywhere we looked. On two successive days we dived with ten sharks each day, and on the third day, in a one-hour sortie along the reef, we encountered another five. I was accompanied by Adrian Mitchell, a keen fisherman and State rugby league player, as strong as an ox. Like most people who like fishing, however, he was reluctant to get his feet wet; but he was eventually persuaded to get in the water and I shot some beautiful film of him snorkelling with the sharks.

Something unusual had to be occurring to account for the sharks' presence in such numbers. It was becoming evident that there was a particular time of year when large numbers of the sharks could be found. I had seen whale sharks at other times of the year — July and January — but the biggest numbers were always in the months of March and April.

DOCTOR TURNS FILM-MAKER

There are many things that influence our lives, some great, some trivial. In July 1985 my family and I were making plans to leave Exmouth. I had answered an advertisement for a job in Queensland; they wanted me to start immediately. And then the telephone rang. It was Elizabeth Parer-Cook, wife of the photographer David Parer, calling from ABC Television in Melbourne. She had heard that I had been filming whale sharks: would I be interested in filming footage of the whale sharks to be part of a television documentary?

It was the sort of thing I had dreamed of doing. All thoughts of leaving Exmouth rapidly disappeared, and I started preparing for the following season. I knew I had some long-service leave, so holidays would not be a problem. I needed a 'professional' camera in order to film in 16-mm format, and it would need to be in an underwater housing so that I could film underwater. Organising these things from a remote outpost like Exmouth was certainly a challenge.

I had soon purchased an old Bolex 16-mm camera, organised an underwater housing, and arranged five weeks leave from work, from late March

BELOW: *The author out searching for whale sharks on the waters of Ningaloo.*

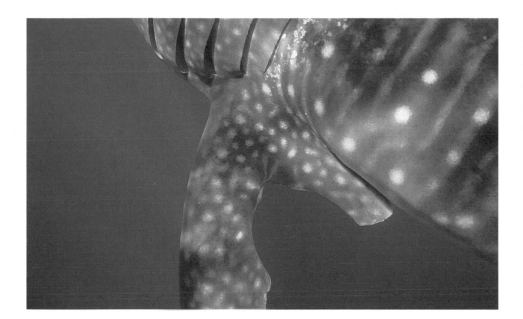

through into April. I enlisted the help of Bill Winchester, a keen American diver. This could be my big chance — to really become an underwater photographer. But would the whale sharks be there?

Here I enlisted the help of mackerel fisherman, Glen MacIntosh. Glen was on the water every day, motoring up and down the reef, fishing for the huge Spanish mackerel. He had sighted a few whale sharks before, but generally took his boat out of the water during late March and April to do an annual 're-fit'. As the whale shark season approached, I checked with Glen on his shark sightings — he hadn't seen any.

Bill and I started searching on 22 March, and the first day were encouraged by our sightings of two sharks. We operated out of the magnificent Turquoise Bay, exploring north and south along the reef. For the first ten days we encountered one or two sharks each day. Then I had to make a week-long trip to Perth, but I returned and continued the search. The weather improved each day and so did the shark numbers. On 16 April we followed a whale shark along the reef for over two hours, diving with it repeatedly. It was not a large shark, about 5 m (16 ft) long, but it was memorable because it had a huge shark bite out of its left pectoral fin, as well as two large gouges down its left flank, possibly from a ship's propeller. I filmed Bill riding on its dorsal fin, and then he filmed me diving down to ride on its back. (This film was to prove invaluable when the same shark was resighted in 1993 (see page 138).) By 19 and 20 April, there were large numbers of whale sharks. We conservatively estimated we saw 11 the first day and 15 the second. As soon as we surfaced from diving with one shark, we would sight another. Sometimes we were even approached by a second shark while still in the water. I succeeded in getting several reels of film.

MAKING THE CONNECTION

It was only at the end of April 1986 that I first learned of the remarkable phenomenon of coral spawning (which is explained on pages 71–2). Staff from the Western Australian Department of National Parks had been at Exmouth to observe the coral spawning at Ningaloo Reef on 3 and 4 April. It struck me immediately that this was a natural occurrence of sufficient magnitude to explain the increases in appearances of the whale sharks. It seemed very unlikely, however, that the sharks were feeding on the minute spawn itself.

The timing of the coral spawning was thought to be related to the full moon, and the theory at that time was that at Ningaloo Reef, there was a three-year cycle: there was one spawning event in each of the first two years, then two spawning events every third year.

RELATIONSHIP BETWEEN PROBABLE DATE OF CORAL SPAWNING AND PEAK SIGHTINGS OF WHALE SHARKS		
Year	**Coral Spawning**	**Peak Whale Shark Sighting**
1983	7 March	14–28 March
	5 April*	
1984	25–26 March	Unknown
1985	15–16 March	7–9 April
1986	6 March?	
	3–4 April	19–20 April

* Extrapolated from available lunar data

BELOW: *Fungia coral spawning on the ocean floor. These coral are mobile and congregate at the time of spawning.*

Researcher Chris Simpson had seen spawning at Dampier Archipelago on 25–26 March 1984, and then again on 15–16 March 1985. Extrapolating backwards, it seemed likely that spawning occurred around 7 March in 1983. From our whale shark sightings in 1983, 1985 and 1986, it was apparent that we were seeing the largest number of sharks two to three weeks after the spawning (see the table above). There seemed to be some sort of problem with 1984 — perhaps we had been searching too late in the season, but according to our hypothesis, there should have been sharks during the three days that we searched.

From the data we'd gathered, a theory slowly evolved: the coral spawning releases massive amounts

of protein into the ocean; this gives a huge boost to the food chain of the reef, causing a bloom of plankton on which the sharks feed. There is a latent period of two to three weeks between the spawning and the feeding during which the food chain of zooplankton builds up.

ABOVE: *A spawning acropora coral. Each polyp becomes engorged as the egg bundle is about to be released.*

If this were the case, then in years when the coral spawned early, the whale sharks would appear earlier, and in years when it spawned late, the peak of sightings would also be late. It would take several more years of observation before we were able to confirm this.

One of the first tasks was to observe the coral spawning events, and plans were made for the 1987 season. On the evening of 21 March 1987, accompanied by local teacher Les Eadon, I ventured out from the shore at Bundegi Reef at dusk. There is something very lonely about keeping vigil surrounded only by the inky blackness of night, waiting for an event such as coral spawning in a tiny inflatable dinghy floating on the ocean. I kept diving down into the darkness to inspect the coral, and it looked the same as always. It was 8.25 p.m., and still nothing had happened. I had promised to be home by 9.00 p.m., but we decided to give it five more minutes. Suddenly, I noticed some tiny pink specks floating on the surface that had not been there before.

Could that be spawn? Two minutes more and the pink specks were everywhere. We grabbed our scuba gear, cameras and home-made lights, and descended to the coral to watch the mass releasing of eggs and sperm. The sight of all that spawn swirling around the coral heads was like an underwater dance, and to see it for the first time was enthralling. As I attempted to film the spectacle, small worms kept crawling into my ears. I made a mental note: 'Wear a hood next year'. When we returned to the surface, it was covered in thick slicks of the spawn. The caviar of the reef had a pungent fishy odour, and it pervaded everything, including our hair.

ABOVE: *Slicks of spawn the morning after the coral spawning. The different colours indicate the spawn of different corals.*

Our searches for the whale shark in 1987 were hampered by bad weather conditions. It was an 'El Niño' year and the skies were frequently overcast. By that stage, most of the town of Exmouth knew that 'the Doc' was interested in the whale sharks, and many people would ring me up to report their sightings. The peak sighting that year was made by George King, the local charter boat operator; returning north along the reef on 5 April he sighted 15 sharks. This was almost exactly two weeks after the coral spawning. I decided that the time had come to document some of these whale shark experiences, and set about writing a paper. It was eventually published in the journal *Western Australian Naturalist* two years later (Taylor, 1989).

A CHANGE OF PACE

Running the big powerboat had certainly taken its toll on the finances, so I decided to make a radical change and buy a sailing boat. I would be able to explore a lot more of the west coast without fuel being a major consideration — far better to spend money on film than fuel. I sold the powerboat, but was unable to find the yacht I needed. It would have to be stable so that an observer could get up the mast. It would also have to be fairly fast, have shallow draught, and be seaworthy of course. I would need to be able to transport it on a trailer. It would therefore have to be a multi-hull. There was only one boat that fitted the bill — a Farrier-designed trimaran, a brilliant design that folds up to go onto a trailer. I started researching these boats. They were almost unheard of in Western Australia. I had only ever seen one, years before in front of Court Yachts in Perth. Richard Court had shown me over the boat and offered to take me for a sail — at the time I hadn't been interested.

I soon gave up looking — there simply weren't any available in Western Australia. It was almost a year later, while driving through a northern suburb of Perth, that I spotted one sitting on a verge looking sadly unused and neglected. The owner was away, but a neighbour put me in touch with him. He rarely used the boat and was willing to sell. It was several months before I could return to Perth to try out the yacht, but in September 1987 an opportunity arose, and he and I had soon done a deal.

Three months later, in January 1988, I drove a 1600-km (960-mile) round trip between Exmouth and Northhampton in 24 hours to meet the owner and pick up the boat. There was no time to sleep; Joanna and I and our three children were straight out on the water. Our sea-trials on the sheltered waters of Coral Bay were exhilarating, and I knew I had made the right decision. I added a ladder up the front of the mast, with a platform about 3 m (10 ft) above the deck. Standing at this height we had a magnificent view. It was particularly good when sailing in the lagoon; we could look down into the water and see all the life on the bottom. Outside the reef, we could spot whale sharks several hundred metres away. Preparations were made for the season, and Allan Sutton, who had worked with me in previous seasons, came back to Exmouth specially to help me on the yacht.

BELOW: *The trimaran* Tribeaut *on the beach at Sandy Bay, with the Cape Range in the background.*

The year 1988 was one when spawning was expected early in March. With the early spawning it was important to see if whale shark numbers in March were different from previous years. The coral spawned on 10–12 March; a second, less intense spawning was witnessed at Bundegi Reef on 9 April. Sure enough, we were able to find up to nine sharks a day in the period from 19–26 March. This seemed to confirm the association between the timing of the spawning and the whale sharks' appearance.

THE MARINE SNAIL PLAGUE

It was around 1988, however, that I found myself becoming increasingly concerned. In 1987 a dramatic discovery had been made on Ningaloo Reef. A massive infestation of the marine snail *Drupella cornus* was discovered. This was destroying the reef in much the same way that the Great Barrier Reef was being destroyed by the crown-of-thorns starfish, *Acanthaster planci*. Small infestations of the snail had been seen before on the reef, but in 1987 it was discovered that huge tracts of coral on the main shallow back reefs had been almost completely wiped out. This destruction was initially worse at the northern end of the reef, but it was to move slowly southward to affect the whole Ningaloo tract.

My first encounter with the devastation caused by the drupella plague was a depressing one. The National Parks Department in Western Australian had invited an underwater photographer, Geoff McKell, to take underwater film footage of the reef for a promotional documentary. They wanted to use some of my whale shark footage, and I was invited to accompany the team on the *Edgar Lefroy*. We motored out from Tantabiddi boat ramp in search of some interesting reef and coral. After a while I suggested we try an area south of Ned's Camp, which I had filmed in 1983. I remembered it as having been a magnificent coral garden, vibrant with fish life. We parked the boat in the lagoon, on the edge of the sand, and snorkelled in over the coral. The whole area had been decimated. It was just like a graveyard, with skeletons of coral limestone covered in a slimy green algae. Only a few sticks of live coral remained and there was hardly a fish to be seen. I felt sick in the stomach as I viewed this scene of devastation.

BELOW: *Drupella snails feeding on the coral.*

Biologists have still not been able to determine the cause of this massive plague at Ningaloo Reef (see Chapter 8). But one thing was certain. Huge areas of the west coast that would normally have been producing spawn were now coral rubble. It was also evident that finding sharks was becoming more and more difficult every year. The seasons of 1989 and 1990 were to be the worst of all.

I bought myself a Nikonos 35-mm camera in 1989, and was keen to get some good still photos of the whale sharks during the season. I had been pursuing the sharks for at least six years but I had only a handful of rather poor still shots, which had been taken with a borrowed camera.

ABOVE: Drupella snails feed on the coral polyps, leaving only the white skeleton of the coral behind.

I had great plans to get some photos for the magazine article I was writing at the time, and organised four weeks' leave in April.

But 1989 was the year when things really appeared to change in terms of shark numbers. A keen underwater photographer, Eve Beaugard, had rung me from Perth: could she come and help look for the sharks, and also take a few photographs? The Japanese photographer Mitsuaki Iwago also contacted me. He was on his way back from filming humpback whales in Hawaii. In three days of searching, we managed to find only one whale shark for Mitsuaki, and despite searching for ten days after the coral spawning on 29–30 March, only two more sightings were made. An air charter company had just begun operating in Exmouth, so I decided to charter a plane and go searching for them from the air.

On 11 April, two weeks after the annual spawning, some friends and I flew down the reef for the first time, and found the whale sharks — there were good numbers of them much further south than in previous years, off Yardie Creek and also off Ningaloo. In 30 minutes, we counted 16 sharks as we flew down the reef, and during the return journey we counted 28. This was probably a world record — nowhere else in the world had anyone seen such a concentration of whale sharks — yet for us, this was the worst season on the northern end of the reef that we had experienced.

From this reconnaissance from the air, I knew that I needed to reach the waters much further south. I was joined once again by Les Eadon, who was an expert sailor and diver. We packed up the yacht, drove down to the southern end of the Cape Range National Park and managed to launch at Pilgramunna on the high tide. For three days we searched, but were defeated by the

ABOVE: *The scene of devastation on the back reef after the drupella plague.*

weather — not rough seas, but a glassy calm surface with overcast skies. It was impossible to see into the water. We trolled a lure south towards Yardie Creek and Les caught a trevally; as the fish came alongside, an inquisitive small whale shark surfaced next to the boat, inspected us, then disappeared. That was to be the only shark we would see on the entire trip. We even took three days to sail down to Ningaloo and back again, but without success. We also took the opportunity to inspect various areas of the reef. The devastation from the drupella snail was obvious everywhere we looked. At the time it was the only explanation we could think of for our failure to find the whale sharks.

As a result of the drupella snail destroying large tracts of coral, the amount of coral spawn produced by the reef system as a whole was greatly diminished. The devastation of the coral was much worse at the northern end of the reef in 1989, although it was slowly moving south towards Coral Bay. Was it coincidence that the main aggregation of whale sharks seemed to have moved southwards in 1989? This movement, plus the general diminishing in the numbers of whale sharks, seemed to be consistent with my published theory that the sharks came to the reef because of the coral spawning. The declining numbers provided more evidence that the theory was correct, but it brought me no joy. The future for the sharks, and for research, looked bleak.

THE RESEARCH
YEARS — THE LEAN YEARS

By 1987, a predictable whale shark season (related to the coral spawning) had been identified. I began to realise that this provided an enormous opportunity to study the species and learn more about its biology. Nowhere else in the world had this been possible.

There were two immediate questions I wanted to answer. Were similar numbers of sharks appearing at the same time right along Ningaloo Reef, or was it always the same group of sharks, simply migrating along the reef? Second, where did the sharks go when they left Ningaloo Reef? In undertaking the research needed to answer these questions, I was assisted by many different people — both family and friends.

To answer the first question, aerial surveys would be required, and the opportunity now existed — Exmouth resident Peter Arscot had just started an air charter business. To answer the second question, we would need to attach a transmitter to a shark. Surely with all the electronic know-how to be found at the nearby Naval Communications Station, we would be able to organise something. Scientists in other parts of the world were tracking whales, basking sharks, camels, kangaroos. To attach a transmitter to our gentle giants would be a relatively simple exercise, we assumed. After all, we could swim right alongside them. In 1987, I approached Geoff Mercer, a manager with National Parks, about carrying out some of this research. I was also fortunate to be put in touch with Professor Gordon Grigg, of the University of Queensland, who had experience with radio- and satellite-tracking. Gordon was full of enthusiasm for the project. And he also had a satellite transmitter that had been recovered from a camel. Together, Geoff, Gordon and I applied to the Australian National Parks and Wildlife Service for research funding for the 1988 season, but we failed to get any money.

BELOW: *Many mysteries surround the whale sharks. Research at Ningaloo in the past few years has helped to resolve some of these, but many questions still remain to be answered.*

The following year Sue Osborne was appointed manager of the newly formed Ningaloo Marine Park. For Sue there were many research priorities far more pressing than the whale sharks, the plague of drupella snail that was destroying the reef being the major one. Geoff Mercer remained supportive of the research proposal but bowed out as principal investigator — I would have to 'go it alone', with Gordon Grigg's support from Sydney. I was warned — the chances of attracting a grant as an unqualified individual were about as remote as photographing a Tasmanian tiger. But I persisted. However, no money was available for 1989 either, and I became disheartened. I decided not to bother the next year.

Then one day late in 1989, the phone rang: 'Where was my application for 1990?' Apparently there was still some money left in the kitty, and a number of people in the eastern states were keen for the whale shark phenomenon to be explored further. There was no time to get a new application together; my instructions were to send last year's proposal with a covering letter. Feeling like Rosencrantz (or Guildenstern) being summoned to the Danish court, I dispatched the previous year's research proposal, and was thrilled when it was accepted.

The funding for the research came through in late January 1990. I was keen to start the aerial surveys immediately, remembering that in late January 1985 I had seen two sharks in one weekend while game-fishing. The first survey flight had to be cancelled, however, as Cyclone Tina came bowling down the west coast on Australia Day (26 January), bringing rain and high winds. Our first flight was on 5 February. I had chosen an altitude of 1200 ft for the surveys, and we found that our visibility was excellent. The view of the coast and the reef was magnificent, turtles and seabirds were easily seen, and we all enjoyed the flight. But as expected, we did not see any whale sharks.

The 1990 surveys were flown using a transect pattern. We flew 5 km (3 miles) due west of the reef on each transect, then flew south to an identifiable feature on the coast. Some parts of the reef are at least 5 km (3 miles) offshore, so on some transects we were more than 10 km (6 miles) offshore. Because of our budget, we could only afford to charter a single-engine plane with fixed undercarriage. On the first flight, as a joke, I took along a pair of diving fins as well as an Emergency Position Indicating Radio Beacon (EPIRB). As we flew out over the

BELOW: *Aerial view looking south towards Point Maud and North Passage, at Coral Bay. The dark area of water in the foreground is Stanley Pool — an unusual pool of deep water in the lagoon.*

ocean, the plane engine occasionally missed a beat. 'Just a sticking valve', the pilot jested. I decided that the EPIRB would remain in my bag on future flights. In the past, I'd always enjoyed flying, even in small planes, but age seems to make us less reckless, and for me, bravado was also tempered by the thought of my three young children. So it was always with a feeling of great relief when we reached the southernmost end of each flight and turned to survey the reef front on the journey home.

On our survey flights that year, we only saw two whale sharks offshore. In subsequent years we confined our flights to the reef front alone. The results of the surveys are discussed in detail on pages 123–8.

The surveys only succeeded to the extent they did because of the fantastic volunteer support from various people. Initially, for everyone involved, there was the thrill of seeing the reef from the air. However, an enormous amount of effort and concentration was required to search the ocean for wildlife; flights could be demanding and tiring. It was particularly important to have a regular survey crew who knew what they were seeing from the air. Novices often initially mistook tiger sharks, and sometimes even elongated fishballs, for whale sharks.

ABOVE: *When conducting aerial surveys, we flew south down the edge of the reef. This aerial view is of the reef south from Norwegian Bay.*

ABOVE: *Pat Willis, Lucy Huckle and the author before a survey flight. Pat and Lucy became regular members of the aerial survey team.*

The assistants included Wildlife ranger Jim Wolfenden, who came on many of the 1991 flights. Battling the terrible cancer, mesothelioma, he showed tremendous courage and was always full of enthusiasm. Sustained by this, he lived far longer than anyone had expected, but eventually succumbed at the end of that year. A group of American families in Exmouth (Navy personnel and their dependants) were keen wildlife enthusiasts, and could be relied on to assist with any research or filming projects. At every opportunity they were there, tagging turtles, helping search for dugongs, spotting humpback whales and whale sharks. Lucy Huckle and Pat Willis, in particular, became regular members of the survey crew, and their husbands often helped search on the water with the trimaran.

I am also greatly indebted to Les Eadon, who assisted with the project in 1989 and 1990. His contribution was invaluable. After our experience of 1989, when we had found most sharks in the southern end of the Cape Range National Park, I was prepared in 1990 to operate from that part of the Park throughout the season. Les had been disappointed in 1989 not to have dived with a whale shark, and was keen to get the opportunity in 1990. He arrived back in Exmouth on 18 March, the night of the coral spawning, and a group of us went in two boats to watch the event at Bundegi Reef. The following night Les and I ventured out on Ningaloo Reef at Tantabiddi in the dinghy, to watch the spawning there. There was one dramatic difference. At Bundegi, numbers of polychaete worms were often attracted to the lights that we used to watch the spawning. But nothing had prepared us for the sight at Tantabiddi: after the spawning, the surface of the ocean was covered with millions of the writhing worms, each about 10 cm (4 in) long. They gathered together in groups, intertwined around each other, and drifted out to sea on the ebbing tide — a rich source of food for the whale sharks.

In 1990 an enormous amount of work also went into developing a suitable pod on which to mount a satellite transmitter. The transmitters weighed 1.2 kg (2½ lb), and would need to be mounted on a platform that would hold the aerial clear of the water. Trials were done with dummy transmitters in a swimming pool and eventually on the ocean. The transmitters were on their way from the United States by sea, but inevitably there were problems, not least of which was getting them cleared by customs. After numerous telephone calls and faxes, they were finally released, but as they contained lithium carbide batteries they could only be transported by road.

We launched the trimaran on 24 March 1990 at Tantabiddi and searched the northern end of the reef, towards Ned's Camp and Milyering, on three occasions, looking for whale sharks. On 29 March we motored and sailed south to Pilgramunna, briefly sighting only one shark. For the next eight days we operated almost daily out of Sandy Bay, motoring south to Yardie Creek each morning and returning under sail with the afternoon sea-breeze. There was someone up the mast on the crow's-nest, looking out for sharks, whenever conditions allowed. At night we camped in a camper-trailer at Sandy Bay. Fish was our staple diet. Every three days we returned to Exmouth to replenish our fuel and food supplies, and to do the aerial surveys. Neither in the air, nor on the water, were we able to locate any decent number of whale sharks. Finally, on 6 April, we sailed back to Ned's Camp, and the following day I searched the area to the north, where whale sharks had been quite common in the early 1980s. At last I found two sharks. Poor Les — he had taken the day off to go fishing. After all his hard work, he had again missed the opportunity to dive with a whale shark.

BELOW: *A whale shark with an entourage of juvenile golden trevally.*

The sharks that were sighted that year quickly disappeared. It was as if they surfaced near the boat for a quick inspection and then dived again. Their behaviour seemed very different from that of previous years, when they had cruised along the surface for much longer periods of time.

Other people had also been searching for the whale sharks in 1990. In mid-March photographer David Doubilet had arrived with Rodney Fox to photograph the sharks, followed in early April by a group of Japanese divers. They were using a spotter plane to find the sharks, and generally managed to find only one each day. They, too, had ended up concentrating their searches to the south, off Ningaloo, and considering the effort of their searching, this was a very poor result. We were also flying weekly aerial surveys of the entire reef, and seeing very few sharks.

Looking back on the 'lean years' of 1989 and 1990, it is hard to be sure what really happened, and why. We know that the main aggregation of sharks in 1989 was off Yardie Creek and Ningaloo, but in 1990 no major aggregation was found. There were rumours that whale sharks were seen at the southern end of the reef, south of Coral Bay.

The year 1990 was my last year of searching for sharks from boats without the aid of spotter planes, and the experiences of my early years at Ningaloo Reef cannot be compared with the four years that followed. Huge numbers of flying hours were clocked up by planes from 1991 to 1994, searching for the sharks.

WITNESSING THE DANCE OF GIANTS

The year 1991 was when I first experienced one of the truly incredible sights of the natural world — a group of whale sharks in a feeding frenzy. Fisherman Andy Young of Onslow had described this amazing sight to me in 1989. On two separate occasions, both in early April (of 1985 and 1988), he had been travelling along the Ningaloo Reef as dusk fell when large numbers of whale sharks had suddenly appeared, all in a feeding frenzy. He estimated there were at least 70 on each occasion, charging around on the surface of the ocean with most of their backs and their large dorsal fins out of the water, their tails flopping from side to side like excited dogs.

It was not until 1991 that I finally saw this extraordinary phenomenon for myself. I had discussed my interest in the sharks with Exmouth fisherman Andy Cassidy on several occasions. One night, I got a phone call from Danny, his son. He had been returning home along the reef at dusk and had witnessed the feeding frenzy. He was so excited about it that he was going out again the next night to see if it happened again — did I want to come? Yes, for sure, the whole family wanted to come.

The sea was almost completely flat and calm as we motored along outside the reef to the area north of Ned's Camp, where a lot of whale sharks

had been seen from the air earlier in the day. The sun was almost touching the horizon when we saw the first animal breaking the surface, and then it was gone. Then another appeared, then another, the glow of the setting sun catching their dorsal fins. Soon they were all around us, charging forward, each creating a large bow wave. Joanna sighted one whale shark towing a satellite transmitter. I raced around the boat trying to photograph them, but it was very difficult in the fading light. Tiny creatures leapt out of the water in front of the sharks' giant mouths, endeavouring to escape. In some places the sharks were moving in groups, twisting and turning together, their tails thrashing the water — a dance of giants.

We were so thrilled with what we had witnessed that the following night, we all went out again. The conditions were almost identical, but nothing happened and, disappointed, we returned home. Such is the nature of watching whale sharks — fantastic highs, and enormous disappointments.

The sighting of the whale shark feeding frenzy was undoubtedly one of the highlights of all my years of watching whale sharks. Seeing so many of these creatures together at one time reinforced the fact that, really, we know so very little about the ocean and its inhabitants. As human observers, we can only catch glimpses of these creatures of the deep — small pieces in a huge jigsaw puzzle that we cannot hope to complete.

ABOVE: *A whale shark feeding at the surface arches its back to gulp the surface waters and take in plankton.*

CHAPTER 6

THE MAKING OF A DOCUMENTARY

S*ome people believe that their lives are controlled by a divine hand. For lesser mortals, such as myself, it has always seemed that a series of accidents and coincidences has determined my path. As a keen amateur photographer with a passion for wildlife, I could not have foreseen that I would become involved in underwater filming and the making of television documentaries.*

FROM SUPER-8 TO 16-MM — FROM AMATEUR TO PROFESSIONAL

There is no doubt that my serious involvement with the sharks is due to the film-making couple, David Parer and Elizabeth Parer-Cook, whom I have never met, and who probably don't realise how dramatically that telephone call in 1985 changed the direction of my life. It was Elizabeth's phone call that kept my family in Exmouth, and it was David's encouragement with underwater filming that set me on the path to becoming an underwater photographer. (Mutual friend, Patrick Baker, of the Western Australian Museum, had told the Parers of my film work with whale sharks.) And their influence was to continue. I tried to persuade them that the whale sharks were a subject for an entire documentary. But the Parers had other plans, and went on to make the fantastic documentary 'Wolves of the Sea' (1988), about the killer whales. Working on my own meant I would have to strive a lot longer to achieve my goal. In the process, I achieved much more.

In retrospect it seems ridiculous, in this day and age, for a complete amateur to think that he could enter the world of professional film-makers. Such dreams could only be countenanced in a remote outpost such as Exmouth. But in fact, many Australian underwater cinephotographers originally started out in a similar way, with an old clockwork 16-mm cinecamera.

PREVIOUS PAGE: *Tony Bomford, an English cinephotographer, getting footage of the whale sharks for the television documentary, 'Dinosaur of the Deep: Whale Shark'.*

BELOW: *Some years at Ningaloo, the water has a crystal clear visibility.*

My interest in the sharks had originally been purely photographic, so it was incredible to be in this position, taking underwater footage that was unique in the world. By 1987 I had built up quite a library of film, and when BBC Television in Bristol, England, needed whale shark footage for a documentary about the Red Sea, they contacted me. The word was spreading. I knew that my amateurish efforts would count for nothing unless I had a considerable amount of film of an exceptional quality. The only other advantage I had was that after several years of diving at Ningaloo, I could predict the best time for filming. However, once I published the data I had collected on the shark sightings, I would lose that advantage. I decided that the time had come to try to interest film-makers in my whale

shark documentary idea. There was always the possibility that once they knew about the whale sharks, they would come anyway and make their own. It was a risk I would have to take.

My first sorties into this media world were almost as daunting as my adventures in the underwater world, and I was soon warned that there were just as many sharks to be encountered there as in the water. It is a law unto itself. There is tremendous competition among organisations to find new material for documentaries. When, for instance, large schools of hammerhead sharks were found cruising around the underwater sea mounds of the Sea of Cortez, off the west coast of Mexico, the race was on to get the best footage and then to get the documentaries to air before competitors did. And to some extent, the race is won and lost in the boardrooms of the television and film companies in the major cities of the world.

ABOVE: *Some whale sharks are indifferent to divers. This female shark was a delight, swimming around the divers on this particular occasion for almost an hour.*

CONTACTS, MEETINGS, PROMISES ... BUT NO PROJECTS

In 1987 I approached film-maker David Moore, who lived in Perth, to find out if he was interested in making a documentary about the whale sharks. David had recently made an excellent 13-part wildlife documentary for television, which was marketed widely overseas but, sadly, never seen in Australia. David was full of enthusiasm but thought the chances of raising the money in Australia were slim. Still, we had a go at getting our foot in the door, applying for money from the Western Australian Film Council, but we were unsuccessful.

In 1988 I took some of my footage to London. My sister had contacts in the media world and she was able to put me in touch with an adventurer called Mick Coyne. Mick had made an incredible documentary about canoeing down a river in Iceland — 'Iceland Breakthrough'. He was interested in making an 'adventure movie' about the sharks. They had used ultralight aircraft on the expedition in Iceland and thought that maybe we could search the reef for whale sharks with ultralights. He would try to get the funding together for 1989. I had some reservations about this, as I thought that Ningaloo Reef was such an extraordinary environment that it was worthy of a proper wildlife documentary, rather than an adventure movie.

On that same trip to England, Joanna and I spent a couple of weeks staying with Jo's mother, Barbara, in the Wye Valley. The first night we were there, we went to a dinner party where we were introduced to one of the neighbours, Tony Bomford. Tony turned out to be an experienced wildlife photographer who had worked for the Anglia Television series, *Survival*, and had filmed all over the world. I showed him my whale shark film footage and he was very enthusiastic.

Joanna and I returned to Australia, while Mick Coyne remained optimistic that he would be able to organise the film project for the 1989 season. The months passed, and in March we were all set to go, but at the 11th hour the project was cancelled. In retrospect, I was almost relieved, because there turned out to be so few sharks around that year. But 1989 was also the year that we searched the reef using a spotter plane for the first time, and we had managed to find a large aggregation of sharks once we began using this system of aerial reconnaissance. In May 1989 I spoke to Mick in London — I needed a guarantee from him that the project would go ahead in 1990. However, the film companies were now concerned that we wouldn't be able to find the sharks. I tried my best to reassure him that we would find them provided we used aircraft, and gave him a couple of months to see if he could organise the project. Mick was very upset when he finally rang back to say that he still couldn't get any guarantees of finance and that we would have to abandon the project.

TWO PROJECTS GET UP

Undaunted, I managed to contact Tony Bomford. It was nearly 18 months since our chance meeting, and I wanted to know if he was still interested in the whale sharks. He was more than interested — he said he would come out to Australia to do a 'recce' at the first opportunity.

Tony finally arrived in October 1989, the windiest time of year, with howling afternoon sea-breezes — not the best weather for diving. I wanted to give him a feel for the whole coast, so I organised some leave from work and we drove south to Ningaloo Station, then launched the yacht. Over three days, we sailed through the lagoon back to the northern tip of the Cape, stopping to dive on the coral and to explore some of the reef's features, such as Fraser Island. Tony was thrilled by every wildlife sighting — there were numerous turtles in the water, and we saw several ospreys. He returned to the United Kingdom with some of my film, full of enthusiasm and hoping to raise the finance for the documentary. We would have to plan for 1991.

In 1989 I had also been contacted by Rodney Fox, a diver from South Australia famous for his encounters with the great white sharks. He was trying to organise a trip for the *National Geographic* magazine photographer, David Doubilet, who was doing a feature on Western Australia and wanted to photograph the whale sharks — what would be the best time to come?

BELOW: Photographer David Doubilet came to Ningaloo for the first time in 1990 to photograph the whale sharks.

The word was well and truly out. Mick Coyne had tried to get finance for the documentary from *National Geographic* and an organisation called Discovery, in the States. Soon every documentary-maker in the world would be arriving.

David Doubilet finally made it to Ningaloo Reef in March 1990. Rodney Fox had consulted me on numerous occasions regarding the timing of their visit, but a trip planned for 1989 was cancelled when David Doubilet became ill. Now they were at Exmouth, but only for a nine-day trip. They were using a spotter plane to find the sharks, and generally managing to find one each day. Considering the effort involved in their searching though, this was a very poor result, but it was early in the season.

ABOVE: *A whale shark over the reef. This female shark has many linear markings, as opposed to spots, on her head.*

I finally met up with them on the last day of their visit, at the Exmouth petrol station, refuelling the boat. The question, of course, was: 'Where are the whale sharks?' I was invited to meet with them that night to discuss arrangements for the following year. David Doubilet was keen to come back and do a major feature article on the sharks, which would be written by shark expert Dr Eugenie Clark. David explained that they would be grateful of my assistance, and that he would be interested in covering the planned satellite-tracking of the whale sharks.

At the time I was unsure about whether or not Tony Bomford and I would be trying to make our own documentary. The project was being handled by Frances Berrigan from Cicada Films in London. Tony's opinion was that if Frances could succeed in getting a film crew into Russia, where he had filmed Lake Baikal, she could do anything. In September 1990 I flew to London, and Tony and I visited Anglia Television. It was becoming obvious that the film would not happen in 1991, but there was a definite commitment for 1992.

This meant that I was able to work full-time on the *National Geographic* project, which was planned for March 1991. David Doubilet was bringing a film crew — Graphic Films — with him. They planned to film the sharks with 70-mm format cameras, some of the largest cameras in the world.

1991 — A VISIT
FROM *NATIONAL GEOGRAPHIC*

For the 1991 season, I arranged five weeks leave from work. It was to be one of the most exciting periods of my life, and at times, one of the most exasperating. On the one hand, it was fantastic to be operating from a large charter boat, George King's *Nordon*, with aircraft searching for the sharks and finding them in good numbers. This provided us with the opportunity of getting some excellent photographs and film footage; it also allowed me to pursue my research into the whale sharks. And it was fascinating to meet all the interesting characters of the media world, and especially to meet a terrific lady, one of the world's greatest shark authorities, Dr Eugenie Clark. However, I was soon to learn that there are conflicting interests between doing research and making movies.

The 1991 season started slowly, with very few sharks sighted following the coral spawning on 9–10 March. This was not unusual, but after the lean seasons of 1989 and 1990, it was hard to be confident that the sharks would appear at the northern end of the reef at all. David Doubilet was keen to photograph the sharks in clear, blue water, and we spent long hours searching the reef, trying to accommodate this wish. However, it was early in the season, and the sharks would not oblige, preferring the green water on the reef front.

When we did find the sharks, a small inflatable dinghy was used by the photographic team for the diving. I found it hard to come to terms with this, however, as I had not intended to spend the season sitting on the *Nordon*, watching other divers dive with and photograph the sharks.

I had been encouraged by Gordon Anderson at Australian National Parks and Wildlife Service to start a photographic database on the sharks that season, identifying each animal, but the opportunities for still photography were few. I spent several days during the *National Geographic* shoot on my own trimaran taking photographs, but without a spotter plane it was hard to find the sharks.

Back on the *Nordon*, the film crew only wanted me in the water when I was attempting to harpoon the sharks to attach radio transmitters to them. (This was to track the sharks as part of my research.) As a photographer, I hated having a speargun in my hand when around the sharks, and it proved a lot harder to attach the transmitters than any of us had imagined. We had quickly realised that attaching a harness holding a transmitter to the sharks was fraught with danger — harpooning them was the only option, and I was encountering all sorts of problems, especially swimming around with a loaded speargun in the middle of a large crowd of divers. On one occasion, a photographer, who was swimming backwards while photographing a shark, crashed into me as I was loading the speargun. It was one of those things that happens underwater, where vision is restricted by masks and there is no sound to warn of approaching danger. I would rather have been behind a camera than a speargun, but found few opportunities.

BELOW: *The whale shark is inquisitive, but it will often 'bank' as it approaches a diver to present its tough dorsal skin rather than its soft underbelly.*

Shark researcher Rocky Strong from the United States had also accompanied the photographic team. In the first week Rocky succeeded in attaching an ultrasonic pinger to a whale shark, and for several hours the shark was followed. (The pinger emits a signal that can be detected from the boat, giving the shark's depth and direction.) It allowed the film crew to relocate the shark and film it repeatedly. This was a golden opportunity to track a shark right through the night and observe its movements — it would be a world first. However, the camera team had a problem with a camera and some scuba tanks, so we returned home — the research was abandoned. Rocky only had a few days with us, and did not succeed in attaching another pinger to a shark before his return to the States. A wonderful opportunity had been lost.

There were some truly rewarding moments, however. One morning we found a huge fishball outside the gap in the reef at Tantabiddi. Hundreds of wedge-tailed shearwaters were circling overhead, and small tuna were leaping from the water. A group of us dropped into the water and circled around the huge ball created by millions of fish. A very large manta ray swam overhead and launched itself into the fish. Above, on the surface, the shearwaters dived down to grab a meal. Groups of trevally circled around the fishball, and small groups of tuna swam underneath it, then charged up to the surface through the ball at high speed. Here was the reef food chain in action. Suddenly,

BELOW: *Cinephotographer Tony Bomford confronts a fishball made up of millions of fish. Fishballs are an important part of the food chain at Ningaloo.*

an inquisitive bronze whaler shark was circling me, passing only a few feet away. For a photographer, it is always at moments such as these that the worst thing happens — I ran out of film. Sharks such as bronze whalers are actually quite difficult to film because they are usually shy, unless they are attracted artificially using dead fish and blood. There is little doubt that diving on fishballs can be some of the most exciting diving in the world.

And then, almost as if on cue, two weeks after the spawning, the whale sharks started appearing in large numbers. With the use of the spotter plane we were able to find the main aggregation of sharks each day. The film crew succeeded in getting some footage with their massive underwater camera and departed well pleased. The frustrating saga of my attempts with radio-tracking is related on pages 141–3. By the end of the season, I was physically exhausted and discouraged.

ABOVE: *The spawning of an acropora coral.*

1992 — THE DOCUMENTARY IS MADE

I learnt many lessons from my experiences in 1991, which I was not going to repeat in 1992, when making the documentary. It would be a difficult balancing act, but I was determined that the research would not be compromised by the film project.

Plans for the documentary were put in place, but it seemed that there was still doubt about the finances. As 1992 arrived, there were stories circulating that various other countries were sending film crews — Italy, Japan and the United States — but there was no news from London.

I had booked a large charter boat for the season, but in January the skipper telephoned to say that the Japanese television company NHK wanted to take over the charter on the boat. NHK knew about the sharks because we had tried to get a pre-sale on our own documentary; in fact they were buying some of our footage. But they had also decided to send their own film crew to film the sharks on High-Vision, the latest television format. I telephoned London, but there was still no confirmation. I had to let the charter boat go.

As February approached I decided it was too late to organise anything — it was time to forget about making documentaries. The rest of the world was arriving in any case, and we had missed the boat. And then on 17 February, in the middle of the night, the telephone rang. It was Tony Bomford.

'It's on! Green light! Frances [Berrigan] has pulled it off!'

I couldn't sleep. How could we possibly ever get organised in only six weeks? We didn't even have a suitable boat!

Well, miracles do happen, and on 20 March, when Tony arrived accompanied by Western Australian diver Denis Robinson, who was to be his assistant, everything was just about in place. Four days later, topside photographer Chris Hooke arrived with a group from TV New Zealand. Chris had recently returned from the Persian Gulf, where he had taken some incredible footage of the Gulf War and the destruction of the Kuwaiti oilfields. And finally, Frances Berrigan was amongst us. The team was complete.

I had originally worked out that the coral spawning would occur on 27 March, but I had forgotten to allow for the fact that 1992 was a leap year. There was a high chance it would spawn on 26 March instead, so I suggested we do a trial run to try out the gear. Sure enough, the coral spawned spectacularly at Bundegi Reef that night, and thankfully, we were there to film it. The following night,

as we ventured out onto the calm waters of Exmouth Gulf in my 6-m (20-ft) trimaran, a huge tropical storm was raging over the eastern side of the Gulf. This was a common occurrence in summer, and magnificent lightning illuminated the sky. These storms always tracked southwards down the east coast of the Gulf. Always — but not tonight. As we prepared to dive and film the coral spawning, the wind freshened, and by the time we realised what was happening it was too late to move. It was 'Swiss Family Robinson' revisited — the wind increased to 40 knots, whistling through the rigging of my trimaran, and waves crashed through, eventually washing away the inflatable dinghy. Some of us huddled together on the floor of the trimaran, trying to keep warm. I had every confidence in the boat as this was the second such storm I had

encountered in it. And despite the storm's severity, the intrepid Tony and Denis descended into the dark below to film the spawning. The dedication of wildlife photographers knows no limits.

There is often a hiatus between the coral spawning and the appearance of the whale sharks. Hence we spent two days offshore at the Muiron Islands, diving the reefs and, in particular, visiting the 'cod hole'. This is a reef feeding station, where the limestone reef, in deep water, is covered in thousands of golden cardinalfish. Large potato cod are also frequently seen there. They are so tame that they will feed from a person's hand and allow divers to stroke them. Many other smaller cod and emperor species gather around the divers hoping for a dropped scrap of fish. On one of our dives, a huge moray eel,

ABOVE: *The potato cod is an inquisitive species. It rapidly loses its fear of divers and can be fed by hand. This particular potato cod was upstaged by the arrival of a huge moray eel, who also wanted to be fed by the divers present at the time.*

ABOVE: *A whale shark actively feeding, photographed at dusk. It charges across the surface with most of its back clear of the water, its mouth gaping wide open.*

over 2 m (6 ft) long, appeared from a hole in the reef. As we fed the moray eel by hand, the potato cod, no longer being the centre of attention, looked on in disgust.

It proved to be a spectacular whale shark season, and by the second week of April we had the clearest water I had ever seen on Ningaloo Reef, with 45-m (150-ft) visibility. The sharks turned up on cue in the same week and we were able to dive with up to 12 sharks a day — the film crew was thrilled.

One of the highlights of the season was when we found the sharks feeding at dusk. We knew that if we could film them, it would be the highlight of the documentary. We made several attempts to find them and finally succeeded, on 12 April, 16 days after the coral spawning. It had been one of those incredible days of diving, with 12 sharks encountered. We had photographed all of them, and also succeeded in tagging half of them as part of a population analysis I was undertaking (see pages 137–40 for the findings to date). We motored along the reef at dusk full of optimism, and sure enough, there they were coming up from the depths to feed. We filmed them from the boat and collected plankton samples of their prey.

But what we really wanted was some underwater footage. This was going to be quite an achievement — if we could pull it off. It is difficult enough for divers to communicate underwater in the daylight. To succeed in getting a camera operator and a diver, with a spotlight, alongside a shark at night, and in a suitable position to be able to take film footage, requires little short of a miracle. Yet the following night it all happened. We succeeded in getting Tony and lighting man Ed Jowett in the water alongside a feeding shark, and they filmed some spectacular footage; footage that is a testament to their enormous professional skill.

THE END OF A DREAM?

As the season drew to a close and I returned to my work at the hospital, it was hard to believe that it had really happened. Years of planning and anticipation had finally come to fruition. The making of the documentary had for several years become a goal in itself. As predicted, many other people had come to make their films and gone home again.

The whale sharks have now had worldwide exposure. The question is — will it do them any good?

There was a time when I believed that these documentaries improved people's awareness of the natural world and that this educational process could only ever be beneficial. I rarely stopped to consider that there might be a downside. I also used to believe, naively, that National Parks are created solely to protect the natural environment. However, in a world where the (un)holy dollar calls the tune, this is not always the case.

I can only hope that the increased attention the whale shark has received in recent years will help to make people and governments more aware of these creatures and their habitat at Ningaloo Reef, and that this greater awareness and understanding will be accompanied by actions that help protect and preserve them.

BELOW: *Cinephotographer Tony Bomford diving with a whale shark in crystal clear water brought onto the reef by the Leeuwin Current.*

THE REMARKABLE LIFE OF THE GOLDEN TREVALLY, OR JACK

In the early days of diving with the whale sharks, we were often amused by the antics of the bright yellow fish that dart around in front of the mouth of a shark, riding in the pressure wave the shark creates. Sometimes as many as 20 of these small fish would swim with the shark. We assumed they were a species of pilot fish.

At other times, while swimming out in the deep ocean, I would be adopted by a group of even smaller bright yellow fish that seemed to be looking for a home. For the duration of the dive, they would swim around in front of my mask.

I was amazed to discover one day that these small yellow fish are juveniles of the large trevally species known as the golden trevally (*Gnathanodon speciosus*). (Americans know these fish as jacks.) The juvenile fish adopt larger creatures in the ocean and use them as mobile cover — a place to hide. At the same time, they are able to travel through the sea in search of food and sometimes, no doubt, to eat some titbits from their giant host's table. They are to be found swimming with dugongs, manta rays and whale sharks, and feature in many of the photographs in this book.

As they grow older, the juvenile golden trevally leave their host and swim together in schools. These free-swimming schools are occasionally encountered in the lagoon at Ningaloo Reef.

Soon afterwards, they lose their bright yellow colour and take on their adult colouration, which is much greyer, retaining the yellow only on their fins.

Other schools of juvenile fish, blue and grey in colour, are also encountered when swimming with whale sharks. As yet, these fish are unidentified, but it seems likely that they are another trevally species.

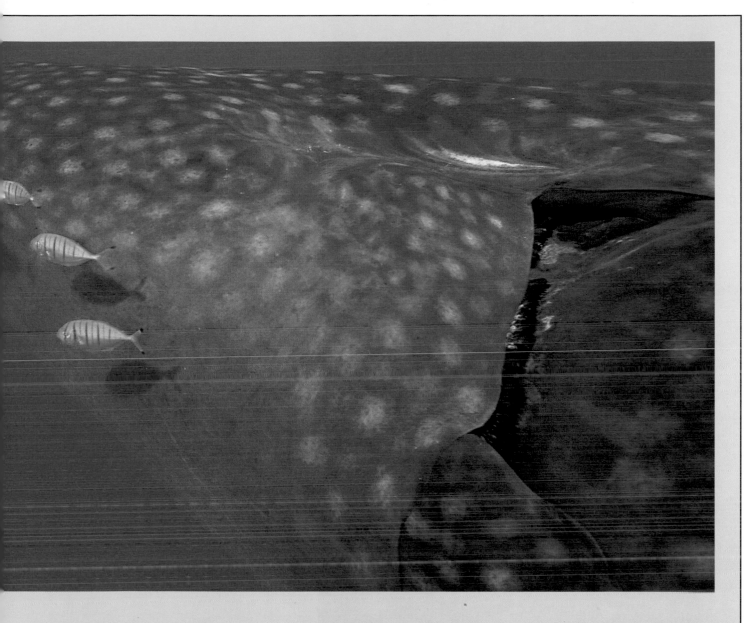

ABOVE: *Golden trevally swimming alongside a whale shark with a badly damaged gill.*

LEFT: *A large school swim with a male dugong over the reef. Slender suckerfish also hitch a ride.*

FAR LEFT: *Swimming in the pressure wave in front of a shark.*

CHAPTER 7

THE
RESEARCH

The discovery of a predictable whale shark season at Ningaloo Reef provided a fantastic opportunity to study the whale shark. It was an opportunity that did not exist anywhere else in the world. With the help of a group of dedicated volunteers — family and friends — and using methods such as aerial surveys, satellite tracking and tagging, I began collecting data to improve our knowledge and understanding of the whale shark.

ESTABLISHING A WHALE SHARK SEASON

Of course these days, the predictable nature of the appearance of large numbers of whale sharks in March and April, and the relationship between this whale shark season and the coral spawning, is largely taken for granted by residents of Exmouth and by divers arriving from around the world to photograph the sharks. It is easy to forget, however, that even the coral spawning phenomenon was not discovered until 1981, on the Great Barrier Reef, and was not witnessed in Western Australia until 1984.

Before the 1980s there had been relatively little boating activity on the west coast of the Cape, especially in the summer months when the coast is subjected to strong sea-breezes and rough seas. As described in Chapter 5 (see pages 90–2), it took several years of searching and observation through the early 1980s to establish that there was a whale shark season. Personal observations of the coral spawning on Bundegi Reef at the northern end of the Exmouth Gulf in 1987 and 1988 finally confirmed that whale shark sightings peaked each year in the ensuing weeks.

However, I still had lingering doubts. I sometimes wondered if the sharks were there on the reef all the time, but were only seen on days when conditions were calm enough for us to venture out in our small craft. There were no planes available so that we could search for the sharks from the air. (In July 1989 these doubts were fuelled by a report from dugong expert, Helene Marsh, that numerous whale sharks had been sighted off the west coast during an aerial survey for dugongs and turtles on 13 July.)

There were other questions that remained unanswered. In the early days, it was generally assumed that the sharks were feeding when cruising on the surface. As they cruise along, they repeatedly open their mouths to suck in water, then expel it through their gills in order to extract the oxygen it contains. In 1986 a shark was filmed feeding with its mouth wide open as it slowly swam along, in much the way that the cold-water basking shark feeds. The question was, were all the other sharks feeding in this 'passive' way until disturbed by the boat or divers? It was hard to be sure. If they weren't feeding, why were they swimming on the surface? Sometimes the water was full of a white planktonic material — known as 'marine snow' to some biologists. At other times, with crystal clear visibility, there didn't seem to be much feed in the water at all.

PREVIOUS PAGE: *Measuring a whale shark's dorsal fin. The height of the dorsal fin is 8–11 per cent of the shark's total body length. It can be measured repeatedly to assess growth.*

BELOW: *A whale shark feeding on the surface at dusk is one of the most exciting sights of the natural world.*

AERIAL SURVEYS

In 1988 pilot Peter Arscot established an air charter company in Exmouth, and for the first time, the opportunity existed to search the reef for whale sharks from the air. The first aerial search for whale sharks was conducted in 1989. It seemed there wasn't going to be a whale shark season that year, as nine days of boat searches had located only one shark in the northern reef area. On 11 April, two weeks after a major coral spawning (on 29–30 March), while flying along 80 km (48 miles) of coast off the northern Ningaloo Reef, 16 whale sharks were sighted on the flight south from Exmouth, and 28 sharks on the return flight. The sharks were mainly located well south, off Yardie Creek and Ningaloo Station. A week later, on 17 April, only four sharks were sighted on a similar flight. It appeared, therefore, that the main aggregation of the sharks occurred at the predicted time of year, but that it was much further south than in the previous six years.

These two flights to search for whale sharks gave us a completely different perspective on the reef and I quickly realised that regular, properly conducted aerial surveys throughout the season would allow us to answer many questions about the sharks' behaviour and, in particular, we would be able

ABOVE: *The survey flights followed the reef, approximately 900 m (2900 ft) offshore. Gaps in the reef spill turbid water out onto the reef front, allowing the currents on the reef front to be assessed. This flight is over the northern end of Ningaloo.*

ABOVE: *Fraser Island, on the lagoon side of the reef at Ningaloo, is now little more than a sand cay.*

to confirm the association between the appearance of large numbers of sharks and the spawning of the coral. In 1989 I was successful in obtaining a research grant from the Australian National Parks and Wildlife Service to carry out these aerial surveys during the following year.

The surveys were conducted from a four-seater Cessna plane flying at an altitude of 1200 ft, with streamers flying off the wingstruts to define an observation area of the reef below that was 500 m (1600 ft) wide. In 1990, the plane flew in a transect pattern up to a distance of 5 km (3 miles) offshore from the reef, then it zigzagged in a southerly direction until reaching Fraser Island, off Ningaloo Station. The plane then flew back along the coast so that a survey of the reef front could be made on the return flight.

In 1991 only the reef front was surveyed, and we were therefore able to extend the surveys south to Coral Bay. In 1992, again only the reef front was surveyed, as far south as Point Cloates.

Our first year of surveys, 1990, was largely unsuccessful in locating the sharks, with only 15 being sighted. However, the negative results that year certainly showed that the sharks were not always there, and in retrospect, the results were useful in determining what conditions the sharks favour.

The surveys in 1991 and 1992 were conducted earlier in the day, and confirmed the timing of the sharks' appearance following the annual coral spawning. In 1991 the sharks started appearing one week after the spawning on 9–10 March, and progressively increased, with the largest numbers being seen on 5 April. A second spawning occurred on 7–8 April, and shark numbers were sustained throughout the next two weeks.

In 1992 when the coral spawned later, there was an increase in shark numbers two weeks after the spawning of 26–27 March, and then the numbers started to drop. We were taken by surprise when a second, heavy spawning of many of the west coast reefs occurred on 24–25 April; the biggest observed aggregation of the sharks was one week later, on 1 May.

These results confirmed that the timing of the whale sharks' appearance is related to the coral spawning. Whether their appearance is as a direct consequence of the spawning is still open to question. What is important is almost certainly the zooplankton food chain. There is evidence that many other species spawn at the same time of year as the corals. For example, at Ningaloo I have observed that some polychaete worms reproduce simultaneously with the corals each year. I believe that the spawning of so many marine creatures at this time of year releases huge amounts of protein into the ocean, and this gives a massive boost to the zooplankton food chain.

Aerial surveys intended to search specifically for the whale shark had never been attempted before. Whale sharks had been sighted during aerial surveys for dugongs in Queensland, Australia (Marsh, 1990) and Kenya (Wolfson, 1986). The sighting of 21 whale sharks along 650 km (405 miles) of Kenyan coast over a two-month period was the largest aggregation reported in the scientific literature from aerial surveys at that time. Off the Queensland coast the whale shark has been seen by Helene Marsh, particularly in November and early December while on dugong surveys (Marsh, 1990). Aggregations have also been reported in the Coral Sea north of Cairns each year, around the time of the November full moon (Macpherson, 1991). (Ben Cropp has reported this too.) This is the time of the annual mass coral spawning on the Great Barrier Reef. The appearance of whale sharks in the Sea of Cortez is now also recognised to be seasonal.

BELOW: *The view from above — a small whale shark in the turbid green water of the reef front.*

Our experience with the aerial surveys followed a learning curve. The 1990 surveys failed to find large numbers of sharks. At the time this seemed to reflect the general trend of declining numbers that we had witnessed over the previous four years. Commercial operators who looked for whale sharks in 1990 also failed to find any significant numbers. This decline seemed to parallel the destruction of the reef, particularly in the northern part, by the marine snail *Drupella cornus*. The two flights conducted in 1989 had suggested that the main aggregation of the sharks had moved further south than in previous years. The failure to find the sharks in the northern area surveyed in 1990 was not thought surprising at the time, as it seemed to reflect this overall trend.

However, we came to realise that the low numbers sighted were partly due to the timing of the surveys, between 2 p.m. and 4 p.m., and the strong afternoon sea-breezes — only 15 sightings were made in the entire 1990 season. From the 1990 and 1991 surveys and other informally collected data, it is now clear that the period between 10 a.m. and 2 p.m. is the optimum time for shark sightings; after this, sightings are less predictable.

Analysis of the data from the seasons of 1991 and 1992 indicates that more sharks are seen on calm days than on days with rough seas, and few are seen on days of heavy cloud cover. Aerial viewing remains good when there is cloud cover, but viewing is very poor from boats. There is little doubt that weather conditions affect numbers seen. Strong afternoon sea-breezes can also affect results.

The aerial surveys allowed us to also plot the direction in which each shark travelled, and assess their distribution along the reef. In 1985, most sharks were seen swimming north, giving the impression that they were migrating north to warmer waters for the winter. However, the surveys have provided no evidence of an overall south-to-north movement along the reef. In the early part of the 1991 and the 1992 seasons, the sharks appeared to be distributed right along the reef, whereas later, there appeared to be an aggregation of the sharks in a favoured area. Whether the individual sharks seen along the reef really converge into this aggregation is not known as yet. The surveys also showed that there is no favoured direction of travel by the sharks.

BELOW: *Seen from the air, a shark feeds on a huge fishball over the reef north of Coral Bay. Wedge-tailed shearwaters wheel overhead.*

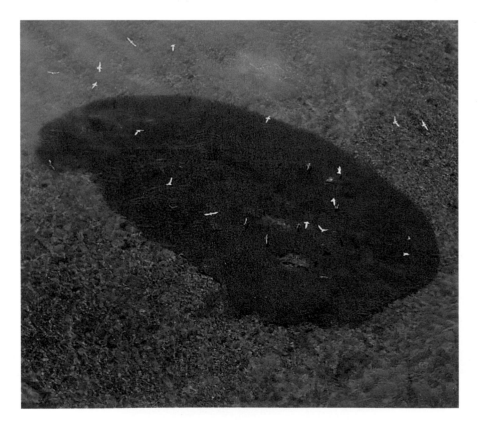

As noted previously, sharks are present on the surface principally between 10 a.m. and 2 p.m. This is the time when the sun's rays best penetrate the water's surface, and it suggests that the sharks are simply basking. The relative absence of sharks on days of high cloud cover or on days of rough seas supports this view. The surface water temperature at this time of year is 26°–27°C (79°–81°F). It is interesting, however, that the surface temperature further offshore, in the Leeuwin Current, is often higher, at 27°–28°C (81°–83°F), so water temperature does not totally account for their presence on the reef front.

ABOVE: *A whale shark ploughs across the surface, intent on feeding.*

The aerial surveys have added greatly to our understanding of the diversity and richness of marine life in these waters. Many other species have been observed. In particular, baleen whales have been seen each year along the coast, especially in the south, towards Coral Bay. From the air it is difficult to be sure of the species, but they are now thought to be Brydes whales. In 1991, four days after the March spawning, the whales were witnessed feeding on huge fishballs on the reef front just north of Coral Bay. They rolled on their sides as they attacked the fish, opening their cavernous mouths. Huge numbers of sharks also joined in the feast, along with wedge-tailed shearwaters, which are able to dive underwater to attack the fishball.

Another interesting finding is the schooling of manta rays that occurs on the reef front during the mid-winter months of June and July. The rays swim together in groups of 20 or more, following each other, head to tail, up and down the reef front, feeding on the blooms of plankton. Manta rays are also seen scattered along the reef during the whale shark season, but they do not remain on the surface. Also during the whale shark season, schools of a smaller mobulid ray can frequently be seen. They have been witnessed feeding on krill.

ABOVE: *A feeding manta ray displays its huge gills.*

The aerial surveys at Ningaloo Reef have only scratched the surface of what is known about this exciting and complex marine ecosystem. The original objective was to investigate the relationship between the annual coral spawning and the appearance of large numbers of whale sharks. Funding was not available to look for whale sharks outside the whale shark season. However, in 1990, we were able to conduct surveys through early winter up until July, and in 1992, the surveys were continued through until early August. Although Helene Marsh had reported sighting numerous whale sharks offshore from the reef in July 1989, we did not find any evidence of them during our reef-front surveys after May. Large numbers of manta rays were seen in the mid-winter months, but no whale sharks.

Nowadays, because of the interest in Ningaloo Reef amongst divers and tourists, there are spotter planes searching the reef for whale sharks on a daily basis. This increased level of observation, combined with further surveys may, in the future, indeed reveal that the whale sharks are present in the area for much longer than we currently believe.

CORAL SPAWNING

Our knowledge of the coral spawning phenomenon (which is explained on pages 71–2) has increased with every season, and it is evident that 'split spawning' (that is, spawning that occurs in two consecutive months) is the rule rather than the exception. Different sections of reef along the coast follow different patterns of spawning. For instance, the Bundegi Reef in Exmouth Gulf usually spawns heavily after the March full moon, whereas at Coral Bay the spawning has often been much heavier after the April full moon. During the three years of the aerial study, the patterns appear to have changed. In 1992, heavy spawning occurred on some reefs late in April.

Slicks of coral spawn have been studied on the Great Barrier Reef using aerial surveys (Oliver and Willis, 1987) and we hoped to do the same at Ningaloo. However, on Ningaloo Reef, we have found that the coral spawn slicks disperse rapidly, if they form at all. In areas of reef where there is a lot of water movement, such as at Tantabiddi, coral spawn slicks do not form at all, even after heavy spawning. They only occur where there is little water movement, as at Coral Bay, and they rapidly disperse once carried out of the lagoon by tidal currents. Hence, the presence or absence of slicks could not be used to monitor the distribution and extent of coral spawning.

From the air, slicks are frequently sighted, but they are generally not due to coral spawn. The commonest slicks on Ningaloo Reef are caused by the algae Trichodesmium, which blooms each summer as the temperature of the water rises. It particularly thrives in Exmouth Gulf, and large slicks stream down the west coast on the Leeuwin Current. Slicks have also been observed after spring low tides; these are thought to be due to a protective mucus being secreted by exposed corals.

The morning after a heavy reef spawning, the surface of the sea is covered in an oily sheen, while the water on the surface is milky with the huge amount of protein it now contains. This rich soup is food for the zooplankton and small fish alike. Within two weeks, the surface has become thick with small fish. They aggregate together for protection, form fishballs and shelter under floating

BELOW: *Two weeks after the spawning, small fish cover the water surface, forming into fishballs or sheltering under floating seaweed, like these schools of 'smelts', hiding under rafts of sargassum weed.*

seaweed or above the reef. In the last two years we have found that some fishballs aggregate over particular reef outcrops. The reefs they choose are always covered with a carpet of large numbers of golden cardinalfish. These outcrops attract huge quantities of fish-life and appear to be major feeding stations for pelagic species, including the whale sharks.

Studies on the Great Barrier Reef have shown that many other species spawn at the same time as the corals. Each year the number of species identified as spawning increases. Every year at Ningaloo, we have observed the spawning of thousands of polychaete worms. They transform themselves into a sexual 'epitokous' form, leave their burrows and swarm to the surface to mate, later rupturing to release their fertilised eggs. The surface of the ocean on some coral spawning nights is covered with their writhing forms. In some parts of the world these worms are considered a delicacy. They may also be a source of food for the sharks.

BELOW: *A dorsal fin is the only indication of a lone shark, feeding on a fishball amidst a flock of wedge-tailed shearwaters.*

FEEDING

Two different feeding behaviours have been witnessed at Ningaloo — passive and active. Whale sharks have been seen on several occasions cruising slowly along the reef with mouths agape, feeding in a passive fashion. There has always been controversy as to whether the sharks might feed on coral spawn itself. Immediately after a heavy spawning, large numbers of sharks are often observed. In 1994, the day after the spawning, sharks were seen feeding passively on the surface laden with spawn. It is not certain whether the sharks were targeting the spawn or copepods caught in plankton trawls. It is increasingly evident that they are opportunistic feeders, feeding whenever suitable food presents itself. They often ingest aurelia jellyfish, but there is no evidence that they actually target schools of the jellyfish.

It was not until 1991 that whale sharks were seen feeding more actively on swarms of zooplankton. Initially, individual sharks were seen during the daytime, right on the surface, dorsal fins cutting the water, swimming through swarms of the tropical krill (euphausiid), *Pseudeuphausia latifrons*. The swarms appeared on the surface as oily pink slicks, and were first seen on 22 March, 13 days after the coral spawning. Samples of the krill showed that they were laden with eggs and were themselves spawning. In 1992 swarms of krill were seen in the first week following the late March spawning.

A group of huge whale sharks in a feeding frenzy is an extraordinary sight. It has been witnessed by observers principally at dusk, but probably continues into the night. The sharks charge around with most of their back and the large dorsal fin out of the water, their tails flopping from side to side. As a group, they twist and turn, manoeuvring to catch their prey.

This phenomenon was first reported to me by fisherman Andrew Young, of Onslow. I witnessed whale sharks in a feeding frenzy for the first time in 1991, and again in 1992. It seems probable that the occurrence of this phenomenon is determined by the timing of the zooplankton's vertical migration. It is also likely that the sharks frequently feed on the surface at night, when it is almost impossible to locate them once the light has gone.

In 1992 we began conducting plankton trawls at night where some

BELOW: *Megalopa-stage larvae of portunid crabs.*

whale sharks were feeding to try to determine the make-up of their diet. There are many problems associated with plankton trawls and the catch is not always truly representative of what is in the water. Fast-swimming species such as krill are good at avoiding the trawl net. We caught large numbers of megalopa-stage crab larvae and stomatopod larvae, but there were very few of the krill that we had been expecting to find. Nor did underwater photography of the feeding sharks that night show the presence of krill. And yet on one occasion, the net was almost swallowed by a feeding shark as it swam past the back of the boat with its mouth agape, so we knew that the creatures we were catching were representative of their diet.

ABOVE: *Diving in a layer of tropical krill,* Pseudeuphausia latifrons, *which were attracted to our lights. Small fish were feeding on the krill, but they seemed to be bombarding us, crashing into us in their confusion.*

The crab larvae have since been identified as being from the family Portunidae; swimming crabs whose rear legs have adapted as paddles. It is very likely that these are the larvae of the blue crab (*Portunus pelagicus*), found in prolific numbers in Exmouth Gulf, in association with stomatopod species.

We finally located the krill in 1992, on 23 August at 8.30 p.m., when a layer was noted at a depth of 8–9 m (26–29 ft). We dived down into the inky blackness to identify the creatures causing the layer, and sure enough, they were the krill. I was surprised that they were attracted to our lights. As we filmed and photographed them, we were bombarded by confused fish who crashed into us as they attacked the swarm of krill.

In 1990 a report was received of a prawn trawler colliding with a large object on the night of 18 June, near Sunday Island in the north of Exmouth Gulf. Shortly afterwards, a whale shark was seen by a neighbouring boat floating, apparently dead, with a large section of its back removed. According to the crews of trawlers, it is quite common to hit objects at night which are usually not identified. Later the same year a report was received of two whale sharks that approached a boat fishing off the Monte Bello Islands at 11 p.m. on 4 October. The sharks came right alongside the boat.

The evidence at Ningaloo suggests that the whale sharks mainly feed at night, when the zooplankton in the water column rises to the surface. Such a feeding pattern helps to explain why the whale shark is so rarely seen throughout the world's oceans.

THE LEEUWIN CURRENT
AND THE CORAL SPAWNING

The Leeuwin Current is a surface current of warm tropical water that flows south down the west coast of Australia (against the cold, northward current of polar water), warming the coastal waters and maintaining the temperatures necessary for coral growth.

By observing the direction of turbid water flowing through gaps in the reef, it has been possible to assess the direction of the current along the reef front, both from boats and particularly from the air during aerial surveys. I was initially surprised, therefore, to discover that there was generally a northward current flowing along the reef front throughout late March and early April. This was first observed as early as 1986, and has been confirmed each year using both methods of observation.

However, the aerial surveys also made it clear that the Leeuwin Current was pushing south strongly about 2 km (1¼ miles) offshore from the reef, heaping up the waves in a wind-against-tide phenomenon. The interface between the relatively turbid green water on the reef front and the clearer water pushing south offshore could also be seen.

The data from a satellite transmitter that became detached from a whale shark provided further evidence of this. The transmitter travelled north along the reef front to the northern tip of the North-West Cape, where it appeared to stay in an eddy for 24 hours. It was then taken south by the main stream of the Leeuwin Current, travelling at a speed of 0.9 knots, as far as Coral Bay, when an eddy took it closer inshore. For the next two days, it travelled north again along the reef front.

BELOW: *Satellite images of the coast show the Leeuwin Current bringing warm tropical water south (indicated in red: 28°C (82°F)). Cooler water can be seen streaming north along the coast during April (bottom) to form a countercurrent (indicated in green: 26°C (78°F)).*

N11/12523
1 Mar 91

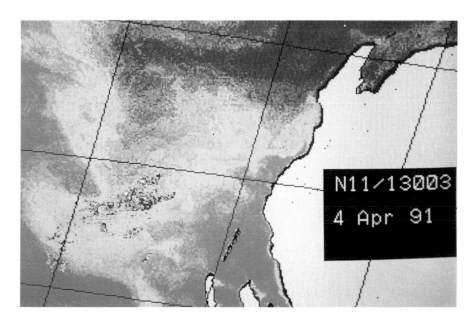

N11/13003
4 Apr 91

ABOVE: *A magnificent faviid, or brain, coral with acroporas behind. The current systems at Ningaloo play a vital role in maintaining the reef by keeping nutrients and proteins within the reef system.*

This pattern of eddy and northward flow can be seen clearly in a satellite photo taken by scientists from the Commonwealth Scientific and Industrial Research Organisation (CSIRO) in the same period (see the bottom photo on the previous page). Our observations off the northern reef suggest that the reef front current finally reverses in mid-April and flows south. The satellite transmitter started moving south again off Coral Bay on 23 April, when it was taken south towards Cape Cuvier.

The north-flowing countercurrent of late March and early April is probably very important in maintaining Ningaloo Reef. As already discussed (see page 64), coral reefs exist in an environment short of protein and nutrients. A huge amount of the corals' energy and protein is invested in its annual spawning. If all this spawn were transported south on the Leeuwin Current, it would do little for the protein balance of the reef, which would rapidly become depleted. However, the countercurrent disseminates spawn and zooplankton rapidly throughout the whole reef system, then 'recycles' it back along the reef front; this is probably essential to the reef's survival. It may also be the reason for the food chain on the reef front being so prolific at this time of year.

The timing of coral spawning on the reef may in fact be determined by this countercurrent system. Corals that spawn when the countercurrent is not operating have simply not survived at Ningaloo Reef, as their spawn has been swept away. Through natural selection, corals that spawn during March and April, when the countercurrent is operating, have survived.

UPWELLINGS

It has been suggested by some authorities that the presence of the huge planktonic bloom, and the whale sharks, at Ningaloo Reef indicates that there must be upwellings of nutrient-rich water at this time of year. On the west coast of other continents there are upwellings of cold, nutrient-rich, polar water, which support thriving fisheries. For this reason there has been extensive research by the CSIRO along the Western Australian coast to locate similar upwellings, but scientists have not been able to find any evidence to date. The sea-surface temperatures of the whole west coast are now monitored continuously with satellite photography.

There are various causes of upwellings: some of the right conditions exist at Ningaloo. The continental shelf comes closer to the mainland at the northern end of the reef than anywhere else on the coast, rising steeply from huge depths. April is one time of year when the area is subjected to strong easterly winds, which blow offshore mainly at night and in the mornings. These are capable of generating upwellings by blowing the surface waters away from the reef, thus drawing up the deeper water. However, the whale sharks are found in the waters close to the reef front, not in the deeper waters 8 km (5 miles) offshore at the edge of the continental shelf, where upwellings might occur.

Oceanographic studies have hitherto failed to find evidence of such upwellings, and satellite photos of the region do not indicate colder water reaching the surface. The evidence at Ningaloo Reef suggests that it is the reef spawning that generates the protein for this food bonanza, producing a rich soup of planktonic life on which the whale sharks (and many other species) feed. Further evidence supporting this is that there is also a whale shark season on the Great Barrier Reef. The season occurs each November, following the annual coral spawning there.

BELOW: *Rainbows in the surf. An offshore wind and huge swells combine to create this. One question still to be answered is whether the offshore winds in April are creating upwellings, bringing nutrients to the reef.*

ABOVE: *A whale shark with an entourage of golden trevally, or jacks.*

SENSORY SYSTEM

It seems incredible that the largest fish in the ocean sustains itself by feeding on such small creatures. How the sharks locate their minute prey in the dark is not clear, but like other sharks, they have a very definite lateral line of sensory 'pores', where their vibration sensory system is located. The pores of the lateral line can clearly be seen running along the body, rising up over the dorsum of the gill slits and passing onto the top of the head. Further lines of pores can be seen under the shark's mouth. Around the shark's head there are larger pores, known as the 'ampullae of Lorenzini'. These pores make up the electromagnetic sensory system, which is capable of detecting changes in magnetic fields as well as the minute electrical currents generated by the movement of fish.

Our studies at Ningaloo suggest that, for the most part, it is a nocturnal feeder, and that vision is probably not an important sense — it has very small eyes. It is likely that it relies on other senses, such as its electromagnetic system, and chemical stimuli to locate the small prey on which it feeds.

IDENTIFICATION OF THE WHALE SHARK POPULATION

Shark Markings and Age

Photography has confirmed that the intricate pattern of lateral markings behind the five gill slits is like a fingerprint, unique to the individual shark. The markings show consistent variation, making them suitable for the purposes of identification and analysis. Some sharks also carry huge scars from encounters with ships or predatory sharks in their youth, which also make them immediately recognisable.

There is now a photographic and measuring program at Ningaloo Reef. In 1992, 44 sharks were identified. In 1993 a further 24 sharks were added to the list, with several resightings from the previous year. In 1994 over 50 sharks were added to the database. This program has made it clear that the same sharks are appearing each year; the opportunity therefore exists to monitor the growth of individual animals.

At present I am measuring the dorsal fins of the sharks as a parameter of growth. The dorsal fin can be measured repeatedly to assess a shark's growth without causing undue disturbance to the animal. Measurements of dead adult sharks have shown the height of the dorsal fin is approximately 8–11 per cent of the total length of the shark. Initial measurements of live sharks at Ningaloo suggest that the dorsal fin height is generally 8 per cent of total shark length, and that multiplying this figure by 12.5 will give a close approximation of total body length.

It also appears that there may be differences in the markings of male and female sharks, the female sharks having far more lines than spots on their heads. The proportion of females increased significantly in 1994, with 14 per cent being female sharks, as opposed to only 6 per cent in 1992.

BELOW: *Named Scarfin 3, this female whale shark was first identified on 16 April 1994. The lateral markings behind the whale shark's gills are like a fingerprint, unique to the individual shark. As such, they provide a good method of identifying each animal.*

In 1986 a shark with a large bite out of its left pectoral fin was found on the reef front. It also had two huge scars down the left flank. We followed this shark for almost two hours and filmed it repeatedly. When it was relocated in 1993, it was again photographed and the dorsal fin measured. The scars had changed, but the lateral markings confirmed that it was the same animal.

There were two fascinating aspects to this reidentification. First, the two huge gashes down the flank of the shark had completely healed, without any sign of scarring — a testament to the remarkable healing powers of the sharks. Secondly, we were able to estimate the size of the shark and its dorsal fin in 1986 and again in 1993. The dorsal fin has grown from approximately 54 cm (21½ in) to 62.5 cm (25 in) in seven years. Whale sharks are about 60 cm (24 in) long at birth. Most creatures have a phase of rapid growth in their early years, before settling into a more constant rate of growth. It seems likely that this

BELOW: *A whale shark with a bite out of its tail. Such injuries are probably inflicted when the sharks are still very young.*

animal is now at least 25 years old. What is of particular concern is that it is still an adolescent, and sexually immature. The only sexually mature male shark seen at Ningaloo Reef has been estimated at over 9 m (29½ ft) in length. Hence it appears that whale sharks do not reach sexual maturity until they are over 30 years of age. This has major implications for the survival of the species. It also suggests that the sharks may be one of the longest living species on the planet, with a lifespan of over 100 years not unlikely.

ABOVE: *The cloaca of the female whale shark is situated between the pelvic fins. It functions as a combined anus and genital opening.*

Population

In 1992, as a corollary to the photographic study, 25 sharks were tagged. Traditional game-fishing tags were fired into the sharks with a small speargun at close range. The tag was placed in a different position on the body of each shark and the position recorded. As a result, when a tagged shark is resighted in future, the tag position will allow identification of that particular animal.

The tagging during 1992 allowed us to estimate the whale shark population on the reef front. For the first time, I was able to verify that we were indeed seeing new sharks each day and not repeatedly diving with the

LEFT: *The claspers of this mature male whale shark show obvious scarring as a result of usage.*

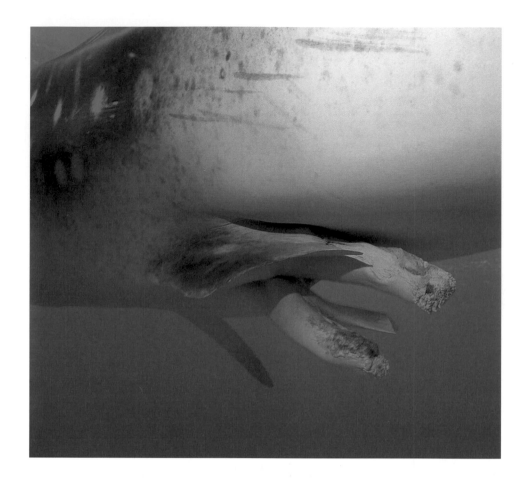

same sharks. Repeat sightings of some sharks were made on successive days on several occasions. However, only one shark was resighted later in the season.

The initial data suggests a population of at least 200 sharks. Data reported by charter boats from the 1993 season suggests a population of 350 to 400 sharks. This assumes that 20 per cent of tags were lost in one year, and that the tags on 20 per cent of animals failed to be recognised. Data from my own resightings, confirmed photographically, gives a lower figure — a population of 200 from 1993 data and 220 from 1994 data.

Sex Distribution

One fascinating finding is that most of the sharks sighted at Ningaloo Reef are immature males. Although usually 6–7.5 m (20–25 ft) long, they are still youngsters and sexually immature. Like other shark species, the male whale shark has two sex organs, known as claspers, inside the pelvic fins. One mature male with large claspers was sighted in 1992, and a few females have been seen — as mentioned previously, in 1994, the proportion of females had increased to 14 per cent. When the large aggregations of sharks at Ningaloo Reef were first discovered, it was thought that they might be gathering to mate. The finding that the majority of sharks are immature males obviously negates this theory.

RADIO-TRACKING

One of earliest questions asked about the whale sharks was, where do they go when they leave Ningaloo Reef? Do they undertake extensive migrations?

In 1982, off the west coast of Scotland, a team of researchers attempted to answer the same question about another species of shark, the basking shark (*Cetorhinus maximus*). They succeeded in harpooning the sharks and connecting UHF radio transmitters to them, one of which remained attached to a shark for 17 days. The data was transmitted to the ARGOS satellite data-collecting system (Priede, 1984).

BELOW: *Joanna swims above a whale shark, holding the small speargun we used for tagging in 1992.*

In 1991 attempts were made by us to attach transmitters to the whale sharks to study their patterns of migration. We also hoped that the transmitters would reveal whether the sharks were feeding on the surface at night. If this were the case, large numbers of signals would be received at night.

In 1991 we had two satellite units, and four VHF units provided by *National Geographic* magazine. These were to be used in our trialling of techniques to attach the transmitters to the sharks. Each satellite unit had a salt-water switch that turned the unit off when underwater, greatly prolonging battery life. A tremendous amount of time was devoted to building 'pods' on which to mount the transmitter units so that they could be towed along behind the sharks. A similar strategy was employed as for the basking shark tracking. The VHF units were used initially: they could be relocated with a portable receiver and directional aerial. This allowed us to relocate the sharks on the reef front to see if our method of attachment was satisfactory.

Many different methods of attaching the transmitters were considered. Dugongs had been successfully tracked in Queensland using a tail peduncle harness, and a similar attachment was considered for the whale sharks. However, the tail peduncle is a highly mobile part of the shark, so chafing of the harness against its skin was likely to be a major problem. Notwithstanding this, attempts were made on two occasions to try this out, but the technique was abandoned because it was too dangerous to attach the units in this way.

It soon became apparent that the only suitable method of attaching a transmitter was to fire a small harpoon into the shark's dorsal fin. However, repeated attempts to do so, even when at point blank range and using the biggest speargun available, only served to confirm what Eugene Gudger had observed some 60 years before — that the whale shark has the toughest skin of any creature on the planet. It was not going to be easy.

Trials with the VHF units showed that if we were able to fire a harpoon into the base of the shark's dorsal fin, a unit could be expected to remain attached to the shark for up to one week. The harpoons were progressively modified, and the firing technique was perfected. All the units that were deployed were retrieved after they became detached from the sharks.

As the season drew to a close, we decided to try to use the satellite units. There seemed a good chance that even in the short amount of time we had left, they would give

BELOW: *A VHF transmitter being towed by a whale shark.*

good behavioural data on the timing of the sharks' surface feeding, and the units would be recoverable if they became detached.

The first satellite unit to be deployed gave signals for the first night, then went quiet for four days before more signals were received. This implied that the unit was still attached and that the shark had not surfaced in that period. The second unit was therefore deployed, also successfully. However, the signals received even on the first night showed that the unit had become detached from the shark and was floating on the surface. It became a current drogue, and the information thus gained was passed on to the CSIRO. The numerous attempts to recover the unit failed; the currents off the reef move quickly and there were inevitable delays in receiving data from the satellite via the United States, so by the time we got to the place in the ocean that had been indicated, the satellite unit was gone.

Meanwhile, the first satellite unit failed to give any further signals after the first week. The reason for this was never clear. The unit was recovered from a beach at Lancelin, north of Perth, where it had been carried by the Leeuwin Current, some three months later. We assumed that the unit was no longer transmitting because it had become flooded. However, when new batteries were fitted, it functioned normally.

This unsuccessful attempt at radio-tracking was extremely disappointing, and is only reported here to illustrate the difficulties that I encountered. It was perhaps the most frustrating period of my involvement with the sharks. Improving technology may make research into the sharks' behaviour and the tracking of their movements easier. It is now hoped that we will get information from 'smart tags' attached to the sharks, tags which can be retrieved when the shark is resighted. These small units are able to store an incredible amount of information for several years. Five tags were deployed by researchers from CSIRO in 1994.

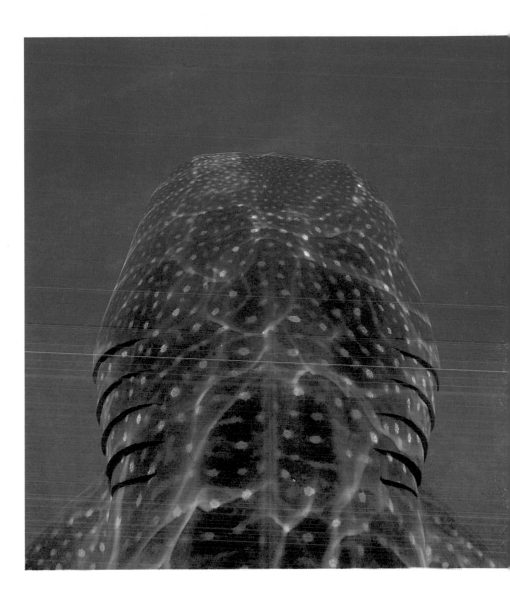

ABOVE: Sunlight sparkles on the head of a whale shark. These markings on the sharks are asymmetrical, and different for each animal.

REPRODUCTION

One of the great puzzles regarding the whale sharks is the question of their method of reproduction. The discovery of a baby whale shark in an egg at 31 fathoms (55 m (183 ft)) by a trawler in the Gulf of Mexico in 1953 suggested that this huge species may in fact be oviparous, or lay eggs. Most other members of the carpet shark family, including the leopard shark (*Stegostoma fasciatum*), lay eggs. However, no other whale shark eggs have been discovered, and it is possible that this specimen was a 'miscarriage'. The whale shark may in fact be ovo-viviparous.

Information gathered in other parts of Western Australia and at Ningaloo Reef has only served to tantalise us more, without providing anything that is really conclusive. In May 1988, while fisherman Bill Johnston was cray-fishing north of Kalbarri, he witnessed what appeared to be a large whale shark giving birth alongside his boat. However, the shark that eventually swam out from below the whale shark was described as 1.2–1.5 m (4–5 ft) long. Baby whale sharks found in the Persian Gulf have been recorded as being 60 cm (24 in)

BELOW: *A school of manta rays, attracted to the reef in mid-winter to feed on the zooplankton.*

long, far smaller than the shark that Bill Johnston described. Certainly, refraction can cause underwater objects to appear magnified, especially when looking down into the water from above, but we will never know what Bill really saw; unfortunately, no one on board had a camera.

In early April 1993, tour operator Tom Jaeger sighted a juvenile whale shark, about 1 m (3¼ ft) long, swimming on the surface 9 km (6 miles) offshore from Exmouth. This is evidence that whale sharks are giving birth in the region.

On 14 March 1991, while conducting an aerial survey, we sighted a large shark swimming north that appeared to have something in the water next to it. We did not normally change our flight plan on survey flights, but this occasion seemed to merit it, so we circled around and descended to 60 m (200 ft) above the water. The large whale shark was surrounded by other, small sharks; there was no mistaking the shape, and the typical movement of the tail. We counted 14 small sharks, swimming in a group around the head of the large whale shark. Whale sharks are commonly accompanied by large black kingfish, or cobia, which can be confused with sharks. However, there are never more than two black kingfish with a whale shark at any one time. From the air the shark looked like a mother with her family of newborn babies, but there was no way of proving that they were baby whale sharks.

Other species of shark are not thought to nurse their young, but on two occasions, bronze whaler sharks have been seen accompanied by what appeared to be baby sharks at Ningaloo Reef. On one of these occasions, three large bronze whalers were sighted swimming together, each with a small shark swimming alongside. I am hopeful that one day, we will find a similar situation — a whale shark that has given birth — while diving, and finally solve one of the ongoing mysteries of the species.

CONCLUSIONS

A prolific food chain exists along the reef front at Ningaloo Reef after the annual mass spawning of the reef in March and April. This food chain attracts whale sharks, baleen whales, manta rays and mobulid rays, all of which feed on the zooplankton. The evidence suggests that the whale sharks move in from deep water to feed on the reef front. During the day they are to be found basking in the warm surface waters. Surface feeding mostly takes place at night, and depends on the vertical migration of the zooplankton in the water column. Identification studies suggest a population of about 200 individuals. The predominance of immature male whale sharks has yet to be explained.

A major discovery is the countercurrent system operating along the reef front. This keeps the protein from the spawning and the zooplankton food chain within the reef system, and may be responsible for the huge build up of the food chain in the area. It is thought that the countercurrent's presence in March and April may determine, through natural selection, the timing of the reef spawning.

WHALE SHARKS AND HUMANS: THE COST OF CONTACT

The whale shark season at Ningaloo has become a phenomenon, with an international reputation. Since 1992, large numbers of divers have visited the area to dive with and photograph the sharks, and during March and April, Ningaloo Reef is a very busy place. Between eight and nine charter boats are out on the water every day, using spotter planes to help locate the sharks. Each charter boat can hold up to 20 divers, although a limit has now been imposed of no more than eight divers being allowed in the water to dive with a shark at any one time. Fears have been expressed, however, that this level of attention could be harmful to the sharks.

ABOVE: *Video cameras have allowed amateur divers to obtain excellent images of whale sharks.*

RIGHT: *The whale shark is generally unperturbed by the presence of small numbers of divers.*

FAR RIGHT: *Two snorkellers use freestyle to keep up with a fast-moving whale shark.*

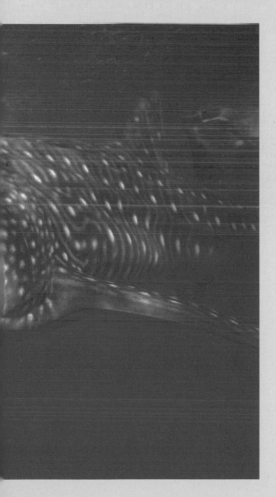

It should be stated that the sharks are unlikely to be harmed in any biological sense. To begin with, the riding and touching of whale sharks is now illegal in Western Australia, so the sharks are not being physically disturbed by aggressive human contact. In addition, their behavioural patterns do not seem to be affected by the presence of people. They are generally not feeding during the daytime, when most divers are around, and the vast majority are too immature to be mating.

There is a possibility that the sharks will learn to completely avoid all contact with divers and boats. The result would be that the whale shark as a tourist resource would disappear, and the tourism industry that has grown up around the Ningaloo region would not be able to sustain itself.

However, the evidence to date suggests that in fact the opposite is happening, and that the whale sharks are becoming more accepting of the presence of humans. This is particularly noticeable with the small whale sharks, 3.5–5 m (12–16 ft) long. In my early days at Ningaloo, they were unapproachable, but now they will spend long periods of time in the company of divers, seemingly enjoying the attention. This lack of wariness of boats and people could have its negative side however — it will make them easy targets if they migrate to waters where they are fished. This is just another reason why further tracking studies should be carried out to better understand the migration patterns of the whale shark.

CHAPTER 8

NINGALOO REEF UNDER THREAT

We now face an unprecedented challenge. Across the globe, human activities are destroying the environment on which we all depend. Natural ecosystems are collapsing, and every day we hear of another species facing extinction. In the marine environment, pollution and overfishing have decimated the marine life of many industrialised nations. In the tropical oceans there is also a crisis — the world is losing its coral reefs.

NATURAL THREATS
TO THE MARINE ENVIRONMENT

When you snorkel over a coral reef or view a photograph of a stand of coral, it is hard to appreciate how dynamic and ever-changing this environment really is, and how fragile. After all, the coral skeleton is made of solid calcium carbonate, and a massive brain coral feels as solid as concrete.

Storm Damage

The prolific acropora corals that grow in the shallow waters of the back reef of Ningaloo Reef are particularly fragile. These young corals may grow at a rate of up to 20 cm (8 in) per year. It is a race for survival and the corals must compete for space on the reef, which changes from year to year. Corals in the shallows on the seaward side of the reef are smashed almost annually by winter storms, and occasionally, a tropical summer cyclone may damage the whole reef front, affecting corals in deeper water. The acropora plate corals are particularly vulnerable, often being turned over by storms.

PREVIOUS PAGE: *A school of surgeonfish over the reef. The ecosystem of the reef is extremely complex, and any disturbance can tip its delicate balance.*

BELOW: *Under the surf — corals subjected to the strong wave action of the reef front 'cling' to the limestone ridges. Thankfully, the drupella snails seem to have been unable to survive here.*

LEFT: *A healthy staghorn acropora coral. Acropora are the fastest growing of the reef-building corals. They grow in profusion on all the reefs of the Indo–Pacific.*

While such storms may temporarily break up the corals, the individual coral polyps survive and continue their growth. In a few years the reef will be thriving again. The Bundegi Reef at the northern end of the Exmouth Gulf was severely damaged by Cyclone Tina in January 1990. Many corals were broken and numerous large plate corals were overturned. However, within a couple of years, little evidence of the damage remained, and Bundegi Reef is still one of the best preserved reefs in the area.

The Marine Snail *Drupella cornus*

While the reef is able to recover quickly from this sort of mechanical damage, the situation is very different when the individual polyps are destroyed. On the Great Barrier Reef, it is well known that the crown-of-thorns starfish has wiped out large tracts of coral, and studies over the past 20 years have failed to find either a cause or a solution.

At Ningaloo Reef the predator that has caused similar damage is much smaller. The marine snail *Drupella cornus*, which grows to 4 cm (1½ in) in length, can be very difficult to find. During the day it hides in colonies underneath the coral. Its presence can be discerned from the distinctive white scar of the naked coral skeleton, where the drupella fed the previous night. Underneath the coral scar the snails can be found hiding, waiting until night to emerge again. The scars are only evident for a few days — green algae quickly grows over the dead coral, disguising the damaged area.

For some reason, during the 1980s this marine snail reached plague proportions at Ningaloo Reef, and by 1987, when the problem was recognised,

ABOVE: *Surgeonfish swim over an underwater garden of acropora plate coral. These corals of the back reef, along with the staghorn corals, are favoured by the drupella snails.*

large areas of the reef had been devastated. The snails favoured the acropora plate and staghorn corals of the shallow back reefs. In many areas, once the coral polyps disappeared, the acropora corals were soon smashed to pieces by wave action, leaving only coral rubble. The destruction started at the northern end of the reef and has moved slowly southwards. On the back reef the destruction was almost total in many areas, with only a few sticks of coral remaining. Acres and acres of coral disappeared.

For visitors to Ningaloo, the magnificent coral gardens of Mandu Mandu were among the most accessible reefs of the west coast; they could be reached easily from the beach. They are now completely destroyed. It is an eerie and depressing experience to snorkel over areas that were once vibrant with life and colour, and survey the skeletons of the dead corals.

Attempting to find a cause for such a phenomenon is like trying to solve a murder mystery — except it's much harder. There are no witnesses to interview and there is no motive. Once they have destroyed the coral, the snails themselves die, having nothing left to feed on.

It is now seven years since the discovery of the drupella plague and we are no closer to knowing the cause. Furthermore, it is now recognised that some of the damage on the Great Barrier Reef that was originally attributed to the crown-of-thorns starfish may have in fact been caused by a drupella species. The question is, are these plagues part of a natural cycle, or are the activities of people to blame?

THE HUMAN THREAT

Many people find it hard to believe that if there had been no human impact, the devastation at Ningaloo would not have occurred. Ningaloo has been relatively free from human interference until the last 25 years, and it is frightening to think that people can have such an effect in such a short time.

Land Degradation

Despite their isolation, Ningaloo Reef and the reefs to its north are threatened in a number of ways. It is interesting to note that one of humanity's most destructive activities on land, the clearance of rainforests, which is happening particularly in the developing world, can have a devastating effect on the marine environment as well. In Western Australia we do not have forests, but there are major erosion problems on the northern pasture lands due to overstocking with sheep and cattle, not to mention the presence of feral animals such as goats. After heavy rains, the huge northern rivers pour tonnes of red 'pindan' dirt into the ocean as the topsoil is washed away, causing a brown slick that floats out to sea for up to 20–30 km (12–18 miles). The silt restricts the sunlight on which the corals depend for growth, and falls in layers of sediment onto the coral. This causes another major stress to our northern coral reefs. Around some of the offshore islands near the mouth of the Ashburton River, little coral can be found. Yet these islands were originally formed by corals. The Leeuwin Current, which is so important in keeping the west coast waters at a temperature in which coral can grow and flourish, brings the silt-laden water down the west coast of Australia, threatening Ningaloo Reef itself.

It is pertinent here to ask, why does Queensland have an offshore barrier reef while Western Australia has a fringing reef? The answer is that because of the high rainfall along the Queensland coast, the corals are unable to grow close to the coast, where the salinity is often low and the rivers pour heavy silt into the ocean. In Western Australia, where there is low rainfall, siltation has not been a problem in the past. But now, the problem of land degradation and the resulting siltation may also be helping to destroy the coral reefs.

BELOW: *An erosion gully on a pastoral lease in the northern part of Ningaloo. The tree has been left suspended in air as the soil is washed away from around its roots.*

BELOW: Melithea squamata, *a gorgonian coral. Gorgonians are a group of sea animals that include the sea whips, sea feathers and sea fans. They are related to the soft-bodied corals.*

Global Warming

Throughout the world, coral reefs are threatened by global warming. Corals grow best in water temperatures of 23°–25°C (73°–77°F). In the eastern Pacific Ocean around the Galapagos Islands, coral reefs were devastated after the El Niño weather pattern from 1982 to 1983 caused elevated sea-surface temperatures. At Ningaloo Reef, water temperatures in winter can fall to as low as 18°C (64°F), while at the end of summer, they may be as high as 27°C (81°F). Any shift in this temperature spectrum could have disastrous results.

Overfishing

One of the activities to have the most immediately obvious impact on the reef is fishing. Every winter, from May to September, large numbers of anglers make an annual pilgrimage to Ningaloo Reef for the magnificent tropical fish species to be found there. Official estimates are that 100 000 kg (220 000 lb) of fish are removed from the reef lagoon annually through commercial fishing and sport. The figure may be much higher: I know of one instance where one boat caught several hundred fish in one night. Most popular of all is the spangled emperor, known in Western Australia as the North-West snapper. Tuskfish, also known as blue-bone, is another popular species.

Marine scientists have argued that there is no data to suggest that there has been any depletion of fish stocks at Ningaloo Reef. But no one did any surveys before people began fishing in the area. Certainly, people can still catch fish, but it should be remembered that modern anglers are very resourceful, and that continual advances in fishing practices and technologies have been made. Long-term residents well remember the days 25 years ago when good-sized 'snapper' were to be caught off the beach anywhere on the east coast of North-West Cape, and Town Beach in Exmouth was a popular fishing spot. In those early days there was no need to visit the west coast for fishing, and even when game-fishing, ample mackerel could be caught trolling up Exmouth Gulf towards Bundegi Reef. Yet by 1982, when I arrived on the Cape, no one dreamed of beach-fishing in the Gulf for the snapper; people travelled to the west coast, where it was still worthwhile. In the mid-1980s most people had their favourite spots for boat-fishing in the reef lagoon, but beach-fishing was definitely declining. By the end of the 1980s, few locals would fish inside the lagoon except at night, and nowadays, most head out to the deeper water off the Muiron Islands. No one beach-fishes at Town Beach, and all the professional mackerel fishing boats have long since left. Yet officials still insist that there is no scientific evidence of a problem with fish stocks, and the opposition from anglers to controls being placed on fishing has been extreme.

It is not hard to see how taking these large amounts of fish from the reef can upset its delicate balance. When we fish, the only fish that we catch are the ones that take a bait — the predatory fish. Other fish are not interested. Hence we deplete the reef system of the predators that normally control the numbers of grazing fish.

Perhaps, for instance, there is a connection between the depletion of fish stocks and the increase in drupella snail numbers. The shell of the adult drupella snail is so tough that it is unlikely that predatory fish would be able to crack it or digest it. However, the drupella snail lays eggs, which would be eaten by fish in normal circumstances. In addition, the larvae from these eggs become free-swimming creatures that drift in the plankton for a part of their early life. It is at this stage that they would be vulnerable to fish predation. Could it be that we have depleted the reef of fish species to such an extent that we have caused this plague?

We may also be upsetting the balance in a much more subtle way. Fish are valued as a high protein food. When we remove large numbers of fish from the reef, we are removing huge quantities of protein and nitrogen from an ecosystem that is desperately short of it. It would seem that these levels can only be sustained if the same amount of protein that is removed from the reef is replaced, imported into it as zooplankton.

BELOW: *A trevally attacking a school of anchovies.*

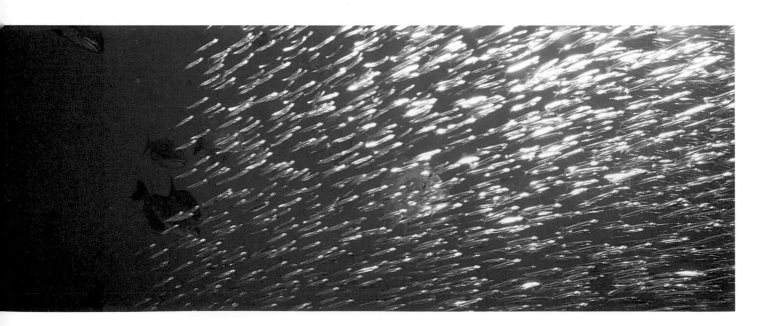

Tourism

A major threat to the reef over which we do have more direct control is tourism. In the past, it was totally unsupervised, and Australian tourists visited the area with an acquisitive philosophy — ready to take as much as they could from the reef, as many fish and shells as they were able to find. It is a paradox that increased international tourism may save the area, for the vast majority of these tourists come armed only with a camera. It is vital that new tourist developments be confined to existing town sites and kept well away from the coral reefs.

A major problem caused by large numbers of tourists is large amounts of sewage, and its disposal. While the surface of the North-West Cape peninsula is dry, the water table is only a few feet underground. There are many engineering problems to be overcome in order to establish a satisfactory system of effluent disposal in such an environment. It is vital that effluent does not reach the sea, for one paradox of the coral reef is that while the whole ecosystem is short of nitrogen, nitrogen enrichment of the water with waste products promotes the growth of algae, which tips the delicate ecological balance against the corals.

One of the jewels of the whole Ningaloo Reef tract is the magnificent Coral Bay, 150 km (90 miles) south of Exmouth. Close to the beach all the corals have died, and there is little doubt that seepage of effluent — with its

ABOVE: *Day's end at Tantabiddi. Numerous charter boats now operate from this anchorage during the annual whale shark season of March and April.*

high nitrogen levels — from septic systems in the area has contributed to this. On two occasions in the last ten years, when there were small tides and minimal surf on the reef to oxygenate the water, waters in the bay were rendered short of oxygen, and thousands of fish died, along with many corals. The excessive nitrogen levels in the water from sewage outfall almost certainly contributed to this, as it has not been seen anywhere else on the coast. Thankfully, the main body of the lagoon corals at Coral Bay has escaped damage from sewage *and* from the drupella plague, and Coral Bay is still well worth a visit.

Coral Bay already has two caravan parks and a hotel, and its population increases by 1500 during the tourist season. However, there are proposals to expand tourist development at Coral Bay with a much larger hotel. Other proposals for hotel developments further north on the coast are also under consideration. One such proposal may be the saviour of Coral Bay — a resort on the old town site of Point Maud. There is a deep water channel here and strong tidal flushing, and it is well away from the threatened corals of Coral Bay itself. There is a good case for all future development to be at this site; a proper sewage treatment plant is also urgently needed at Coral Bay.

If we are not careful, the ever-increasing numbers of tourists will destroy the very environment they have come to see. The whole question of tourist development has been the subject of several government investigations. It seems that such investigations never satisfy the development lobby, who continue their campaign to be granted more and more development opportunities.

The Oil and Shipping Industries

All of the above environmental stresses pale into insignificance before the potential threat from the oil and shipping industries. They continually try to reassure us that they can operate in safety, yet every year throughout the world there are major environmental disasters as a direct result of oil and shipping accidents.

It is sobering to contemplate the scale of accidents that can occur during the phases of oil exploration and production. When the Ixtoc 1 Well in the Gulf of Mexico blew out on 2 June 1979, engineers were unable to cap it for six months. The well spilled up to 30 000 barrels of oil per day into the ocean — there are 159 litres (42 US gallons) of oil in one barrel — creating a slick 960 km (600 miles) long.

BELOW: *Thevenard Island. The offshore islands of the region, which are the last refuge for some mammals, are being taken over by the oil industry.*

The really crucial question in all the debates about the offshore oil industry is, how close is too close? The answer must surely relate to how far oil slicks have travelled in previous disasters. The *Exxon Valdez* disaster in Alaska provides just one example; the oil slick caused by that shipping accident damaged more than 300 miles of coastline.

In the Ningaloo region, the oil industry is currently drilling a field which is a mere 25 km (15 miles) offshore from North-West Cape, to the west of the Muiron Islands. Further offshore (75 km (45 miles) away), the Griffen Field is producing 80 000 barrels of oil a day. Floating above this oil field is an enormous supertanker, called the *Griffen Venture*. Weighing 100 000 tonnes, this vessel is bigger than the *Exxon*, stores 700 000 barrels of oil, and is used as a storage facility for smaller tankers to offload oil. Further south is the highly productive Saladin Field, which is based around Thevenard Island, off Onslow. Individual wells there have recorded oil flows as high as 10 000 barrels a day, making them the most productive in Australia.

On Thursday, 24 February 1994, a huge tug, the *Boaforce*, struck an underwater oil well-head and sank off Thevenard Island. Thankfully, the well-head did not leak any oil, but if it had been productive and the head had been fractured, a disaster similar in proportions to that of the Ixtoc 1 Well in the Gulf of Mexico could well have been the result. The tug was operating in an area officially defined as an environmentally sensitive area (ESA), and was carrying over 200 000 litres (52 000 US gallons) of diesel. Incidents such as these do little to inspire confidence in the industry's ability to avoid disaster in the future.

ABOVE: Mersk Valiant, *an oil rig drilling in Exmouth Gulf.*

Conservation agencies in Western Australia have produced petroleum industry guidelines aimed at protecting the environment and avoiding such disasters. The Western Australian Environmental Protection Agency recently produced a draft document to replace the original guidelines, known as 'Bulletin 104', published in 1984 by the Department of Conservation and Environment. Their strategy is based on a model of marine parks within ESAs, which are protected by buffer zones from open waters. The buffer zones are 30 km (18 miles) wide, the distance an oil slick is likely to travel in 24 hours. This theoretically gives the industry 24 hours to react with containment booms and dispersants to an oil spill.

The concept is superb, and perhaps there exists a 'never-never' land somewhere in the world where it can be put into practice one day. The fact is, however, that for the last two decades in Western Australia, most oil exploration has been occurring within ESAs themselves, so in practice, no buffer zones exist at all. Many of the most productive fields — Barrow Island, the Saladin Field — are well within these ESAs, and the latest field is on the edge of the Ningaloo Marine Park.

In Australian waters the oil industry has a phenomenal safety record for the exploration phase of operations, and has had major successes in locating much-needed oil and gas on the North-West Shelf in recent years. However, the risks of a major spill are far greater during the production and transportation phases, which inevitably involve one of the dirtiest and least regulated industries in the world — the shipping industry.

The realities of this were brought home to Australians when, in July 1991, the Greek tanker, *The Kirke* lost a section of its bow off the coast of Western Australia, just north of Perth, spilling tonnes of oil into the ocean. The beaches and reefs along this stretch of coast were only saved from oil contamination by unusually strong offshore winds. On the night following the disaster, Western Australians were reassured by the media that a disaster would be averted and that the stricken vessel would be towed north (past the entire length of Ningaloo Reef) to the calm waters of Exmouth Gulf, where the remaining oil would be piped into another tanker. Such is the appreciation of the importance of the Ningaloo region by some in the corridors of power!

The thought of such a scenario is even more sobering when it is realised that 75 per cent of the world's oil tanker fleet is over 15 years old, and that many vessels are recognised by the industry as being near the end of their useful life.

On the north-west coast of Australia, the oil industry is pushing the war of technology against the environment to the limits. To expect that such an industry can operate without mishap in a region subject to tropical cyclones is perhaps the height of human arrogance. The oil industry frequently boasts that the North Rankin–A Platform survived one of the strongest cyclones in modern history, Cyclone Orson, with winds exceeding 200 km (120 miles) per hour. It was indeed an engineering feat. At the same time, however, a nearby semi-submersible drilling rig, the Sedco 600, broke loose from its anchors and drifted 32 km (20 miles) from its drill site in horrendous seas. It took six weeks to relocate it over the well-hole. If this rig, careering out of control, had struck another rig, a well-head or a tanker, a major disaster would have occurred.

The industry continually tries to impress and reassure the public with its oil spill contingency plans (OSCPs) — containment booms and dispersants — to cope with a spill. One of the most famous oil disasters occurred in flat, calm waters at a port that the industry had boasted was one of the safest oil terminals in the world. Despite ideal conditions for 24 hours after the *Exxon* went aground at the port of Valdez in Alaska, the oil spill contingency plans were a total failure. What chance would there be of controlling a spill in a tropical storm?

In 1989, a conservation group was set up in Exmouth. It has monitored the activities of the oil industry since then. There is no doubt that tropical cyclones are a major threat to the industry's activities. In dealing with tropical cyclones, the industry relies on accurate weather forecasting. Yet we now know that tropical cyclones obey no laws, except those of chaos theory, and are by their very nature unpredictable. One of the greatest difficulties that the

BELOW: *Damselfish and wrasse over a montipora coral. Studies have shown that corals can be killed by exposure to miniscule concentrations (10 parts per million) of fuel oil, and by even smaller concentrations of oil treated with dispersants. Studies in Panama of an oil-damaged reef have shown little recovery after five years. The recovery is expected to take longer than the lifespan of the investigators.*

weather bureau has is deciding when a tropical depression off the north coast of Australia has in fact become a cyclone. It is interesting to look at some of the occurrences of the last six years.

Cyclone Herbie formed off the coast in May 1988, but it was so late in the cyclone season that a cyclone formation was not initially suspected. And because it had no large mass of cloud, it could not be seen clearly on satellite photos. The salt-carrying ship *Korean Star* had deballasted and was waiting to load at Cape Cuvier, to the south of the Ningaloo Reef. The crew were not overconcerned by the forecast gales but were totally unprepared for the wind strengths that developed. The wreck of the *Korean Star* beneath the cliffs near Cape Cuvier is testament to the unpredictability of weather systems in this part of the world.

When Depression Tina came down the coast on 26 January 1990, the town of Exmouth was preparing for Australia Day celebrations. The depression system had a very large central eye, but the weather bureau was rightly

BELOW: *The* Korean Star *had little warning of the approach of Tropical Cyclone Herbie in 1988, and is now a monument to the unpredictability of the weather systems of northern Australia.*

cautious, and decided to label it a cyclone. The celebrations were cancelled. At midday, the cyclone alert was cancelled; yet an hour later, the town was put on 'red alert'. As the system approached the coast, the winds abated and it was decided that it wasn't a dangerous system; at 7 p.m. all cyclone alerts were cancelled once again. An hour and a half later, the drilling ship *Energy Searcher* 80 km (48 miles) out to sea, was hit by huge 9-m (30-ft) seas on the beam, accompanied by 110-km (70-mile) per hour winds. Six of its eight anchor chains had to be cut with oxy-torches to allow the ship to swing around and head into the wind — a crew member was injured in this operation. The ship was heeling over on a 20-degree angle. It was described as 'a radical situation', and no one was able to advise the ship about what the weather would do next. Thankfully, the wind slowly decreased in strength and disaster was averted.

A month later, Cyclone Vincent travelled south along the coast, about 300 km (180 miles) offshore. Strong winds were not expected on the coast, but they arrived unannounced. An oil tanker, *The Neptune–Otome*, had deballasted to take on oil at the Airlie Island tanker terminal, off Onslow, to the north of Ningaloo Reef. The ship was hit by 110–130-km (70–80-mile) per hour winds and started dragging the anchors. The oil feeder-pipe was parted, spilling oil into the ocean. Fortunately, the ship was blown past Airlie Island and did not run aground, but it was another close call.

The message is simple: we can never afford to be blasé when dealing with tropical storms. Nor can anyone claim that an accident will never happen.

There are many other issues that are of concern, not the least of which is the fact that the oil industry relies on highly toxic chemical dispersants to sink oil in the event of a spill. These dispersants and the resultant oil–dispersant mixture have been shown to be far more toxic than the oil itself. The use of dispersants reflects the 'out of sight, out of mind' attitude of the industry. Once the oil has sunk to the bottom of the ocean, the havoc it causes to the local environment cannot be discerned. Yet oil industry representatives are quite prepared to use dispersants, even in the vicinity of the Marine Park.

Ballast Water

All over the world, people are realising that the marine environment is in trouble — strange changes are occurring to marine ecosystems. The problem is that the huge transport ships — the iron ore carriers, salt carriers and oil tankers — travel the oceans of the world carrying sea water. They are unable to put to sea empty, as they would be unstable, so they take on sea water as ballast and then discharge this water when and where they load their cargo. As a country that exports a lot of primary produce, Australia is one of the largest importers of foreign sea water. It is estimated that 58 million tonnes of foreign sea water is discharged on Australian coasts annually. This sea water contains vast numbers of marine organisms, often the larvae of much larger creatures, which are thus introduced to a new environment.

In Australia there are at least 14 established species that are known to have been introduced by ballast water. These include two species of fish, four species of crustaceans, three species of molluscs, three species of polychaete worms, one seaweed and one toxic dinoflagellate species. Some of these organisms do not have any predators in their new environments to keep them in check and they are therefore able to spread rapidly.

As a result, an Asian starfish and a Japanese seaweed are taking over the coast of Tasmania; Japanese crabs are in Cockburn Sound, off Perth; two species of Asian molluscs are in the Swan River, in Western Australia; several species of Asian gobyfish can be found in the ports along the east coast; and a toxic dinoflagellate, *Gymnodinales*, is affecting mussel and oyster farms in Tasmania.

The introduction of exotic creatures via ballast water has the potential to devastate fragile environments such as coral reefs. It is in fact quite possible that the plague of *Drupella cornus* at Ningaloo Reef is a virulent strain of the marine snail introduced by shipping. While this may seem far-fetched to some, it should not be forgotten that the first description of a reef devastated by a drupella species came from southern Japan. (Genetic studies may confirm or disprove this theory.)

BELOW: *Fishballs of anchovies form over reefs where cardinalfish live. While coral reefs appear to be solid and unchanging, they are in fact dynamic, complex and fragile environments*

STATUS OF THE WORLD'S CORAL REEFS

Some biologists argue that the destruction of coral reefs may be a natural phenomenon that has occurred before — a type of biological purging. Such destruction, they believe, may be the result of several chance events, and perhaps, in the long-term, it may even be beneficial. The experience of the Great Barrier Reef has already shown how powerless we are to influence the course of events, and how difficult it is to find a simple cause — not to mention a solution.

Whatever the cause, it should be a lesson to us that no nation is immune from the problems of the planet. The disappearing reef is yet another example of how our whole environment is changing. It is very easy to focus only on the local problem, but the Ningaloo situation needs to be viewed within the context of all the coral reefs of the South-East Asian region. Everywhere you look, it is the same story — coral reefs that are degraded and disappearing.

In 1992, in Guam, coral reef scientists from around the world gathered at the Seventh International Coral Reef Symposium to discuss the state of the world's coral reefs. The message from that conference was a depressing one. One paper presented there stated:

> *Coral reefs of the world are declining so rapidly that localised exterminations are probable … It is predicted that: 10% of the coral reefs of the world have already been degraded beyond recognition; 30% are in a critical state such that they will be lost in the next 10–20 years; another 30% are threatened and will disappear in 20–40 years; which leaves about 30% which appear stable and which may remain for hundreds to thousands of years (Wilkinson et al, 1993).*

This paper listed many of the stresses on the reefs that result from human activities — anthropogenic stresses. They included sewage, agricultural and industrial run-off, excessive sedimentation from deforestation and land clearing for domestic and agricultural purposes; and overexploitation of the oceans, particularly through overfishing and the use of destructive fishing methods. Other threats included hydrocarbon pollution from oil, pesticides, PCBs and toxic waste materials, as well as heavy metals.

The point is made in the paper that a huge amount of time, effort and money is required to research the marine environment, and it is difficult to produce data with a 'confidence level' that will satisfy marine managers. However, by the time such data *is* available, it is usually already too late to implement management strategies that will achieve what needs to be done. The speed of the destruction at Ningaloo Reef certainly supports this view.

But more importantly, before management strategies are implemented, it is vital that the 'status' of a reef is recognised by government and marine authorities. Only then will adequate resources be made available for research and management of a problem.

ABOVE: *Fungia corals in a cluster on the reef. These corals are mobile and congregate together to spawn at the time of the annual mass reef spawning.*

THE STATUS OF NINGALOO REEF

The Seventh International Coral Reef Symposium took place in June 1992, five years after the drupella plague at Ningaloo Reef was discovered, and seven months after a Western Australian workshop on *Drupella cornus* was held. One paper from the Symposium stated, 'Reefs to the south [that is, in Australia] … are virtually all considered stable'.

So what is the status of Ningaloo Reef? It is pertinent to look at the data from the Western Australian studies on the state of the reef in 1991 and compare it with the figures for other countries in the South-East Asian region (Wilkinson et al, 1993). The techniques for assessing reefs are standard — determining the percentage of cover of live coral. In the South-East Asian studies, reefs were classified as being in poor condition if live coral cover was less than 25 per cent, fair if coral cover was 25–50 per cent, and stable if cover was more than 50 per cent.

At Ningaloo, on the west coast, the most prolific coral growth used to be on the shallow back reefs — probably 80 per cent of the coral biomass was originally there — which extend in an almost unbroken line for 200 km (120 miles).

In a few areas there are stands of coral in the deeper, sheltered waters of the lagoon, and at the lagoon sites studied there was reasonable live coral cover — 43–52 per cent. On the shallow back reef it is a different story, with figures as low as 3.8 per cent at the northern end of the reef. The difference between the coral cover in the lagoon and back reef was well demonstrated at the magnificent Coral Bay — in the lagoon there was 43.7 per cent coral cover, while on the back reef, only 10.63 per cent cover.

There was one notable exception to this trend. At the very southern end of Ningaloo Marine Park, live coral cover in 1991 was as high as 79.8 per cent, but within this coral, 15.95 drupella snails could be found per square metre (yard). The drupella plague had finally reached these southern corals, which were doomed to be destroyed.

Hence, the vast majority of the reef, that is the coral of the back reef, is in the 'poor' category according to the South-East Asian study's classifications — some might even say devastated — and only the few lagoon sites show 'fair' to 'good' cover. It would not be an exaggeration to say that over 80 per cent of the coral biomass has disappeared from the northern reef tract (north of Yardie Creek). And if the reef were classified according to the International Code, it would be in the 'critical' category. Some might try to justify a label of 'threatened', but no one in their right mind could say that the reef was 'stable'. If Australian reefs are currently considered to be the stable reefs of the region, we must seriously question whether any reefs will survive the tremendous environmental pressures expected during the next 40 years.

MANAGING THE MARINE ENVIRONMENT

The marine environment is so complex that it may well be that we will never adequately explain the cause of the drupella snail destruction at Ningaloo Reef nor, equally, the destruction of the Great Barrier Reef by the crown-of-thorns starfish. The belief held in some quarters that such destruction may be part of a natural cycle has bred an inertia on the part of both government and bureaucrats that borders on indifference. Seven years after the drupella problem was discovered, there is still no official recognition that Ningaloo Reef is in trouble, and research into the issue has almost ceased.

Will the reef recover? In some areas of the Great Barrier Reef where the crown-of-thorns starfish caused

BELOW: *Low tide in the mangroves leaves the pneumatophores, or vertical root branches, exposed. The mud that is also revealed is thick with nutrients and nitrogen-fixing organisms — a rich source of nutrients for the whole reef environment.*

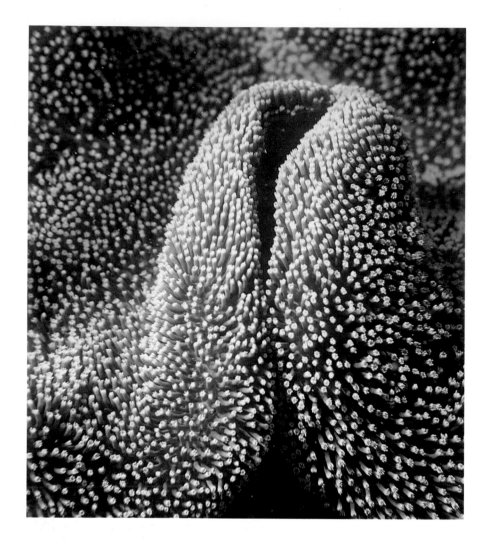

ABOVE: Sarchophyton trocheliophorum, an alcyoniid, or soft coral. Coral reefs, once destroyed, are often taken over by these soft, fast-growing corals, which then prevent the hard, or 'true', corals from regenerating.

damage, there has sometimes been a spectacular recovery in a mere ten years. This occurred at John Brewer Reef for instance, between 1970 and 1980. However, a further plague destroyed the reef again in 1984. In areas where the Great Barrier Reef is under 'chronic stress' from nutrient run-off and tourism, such as at Green Island off Cairns, there has been no recovery from the damage caused by the crown-of-thorn starfish at all.

An inspection of the northern Ningaloo reef in 1994 — seven years after the plague was discovered — showed that at Turquoise Bay, the back reef is being taken over by 'soft corals' and the stinging hydrocoral, *Millepora*. The lagoon corals in the bay are algae-covered skeletons with no sign of recovery. Further north, off Ned's Camp, the back reef has about 1 per cent coral cover. The surviving corals are faviids — no acroporas can be found at all.

As I have already stated, the decline of Ningaloo Reef needs to be considered in the context of the decline of every other reef in the region. If we simply accept the view that the drupella plague is a natural phenomenon, we may fail to optimise conditions for the reef's recovery. There is nothing that anyone can do to remove the snail from the ecosystem. However, if there is any chance at all that overfishing has caused the problem, then surely we should be putting controls in place, to provide far greater protection of the reef fish stocks than those that exist currently. We should be doing all in our power to reduce environmental stress to the reef. The creation of a Marine Park defines a natural resource, which can be marketed to attract tourists. But it is vital that management strategies be put in place to protect that resource. Currently, there are proposals being considered to *increase* tourist development along the coast, and the oil industry is being allowed to operate within 16 km (10 miles) of the reef. (Whatever happened to the buffer zone concept?) If controls are not introduced regarding the discharge of ballast water, and if oil tanker terminals are not located much further out to sea (no one knows what a safe distance for such operations is), it is highly likely that there will be an ecological disaster.

SURVIVAL OF THE WHALE SHARK

Throughout the world, animals and plants are becoming extinct because of the destruction of their habitat. At Ningaloo Reef there are thousands of animals depending on the reef for their survival. The destruction of the back-reef corals at Ningaloo Reef has already caused the disappearance of millions of creatures from these areas. At present, we do not have a complete understanding of how dependent the whale shark may be on this unique environment, so we do not know if its survival is threatened.

The official conservation status of the whale shark is currently 'unknown'. While in the Australian region the whale shark would seem to have few predators, in much of the developing world, including neighbouring Indonesia, the whale shark is slaughtered for its meat. As the world's population increases and food shortages become more of a problem, it will be hard for fishing boats to ignore this massive source of protein. Also, it has been found that the liver oil of the whale shark has powerful anti-tumour properties. This too could make the sharks a target for the fishing industry.

At Ningaloo Reef, whale sharks became much more difficult to find during the late 1980s. Since that time spotter planes have been employed by divers to search for them. The planes make it easier to find the whale sharks, but they also make it difficult to determine if the trend towards decreasing numbers has continued.

BELOW: *Snorkellers following a whale shark as it cruises through the ocean.*

FOR THE FUTURE

It is sometimes easier to ignore a problem than to acknowledge it. As long as successive governments fail to recognise the extent of the problem, they may also fail to allocate resources, and more importantly, they may pursue policies that continue to threaten the recovery of Ningaloo Reef.

'Environmentally sustainable development' was a political catch phrase of the 1980s. However, the continued deterioration of ecosystems both on land and at sea has made a mockery of this stance. It is a fact of modern life that 'economic rationalism' controls political decision-making. Ningaloo Reef and the whale sharks will need to 'earn their keep' as a tourism resource before their protection will be given priority over economic development by politicians.

Coral reefs and mangroves are extremely important in forming the basis of the food chains of the tropical oceans. Yet in the tropics, both are fast disappearing. If we do not halt this trend, then much, if not all, of the marine life in the tropical oceans that depend upon them will disappear. We will witness the demise of thousands of species, including, perhaps, such giants as the whale shark.

We now have a great opportunity to preserve Ningaloo Reef, at the same time ensuring that the whale sharks and all the other marine species of the reef continue to thrive. The reef is a fantastic natural wonder, and an enormous natural resource. To preserve it for future generations is the challenge, but if we are to do so, we must act now.

BELOW: *A whale shark cruising through the ocean — what future is there for this extraordinary species?*

BIBLIOGRAPHY

Baughman, J. L. 1955, 'The oviparity of the whale shark, *Rhineodon typus*, with records of this and other fishes in Texan waters', *Copeia*, vol. 1, pp. 54–5.

Boucher, L. M. 1986, 'Coral predation by muricid gastropods of the genus *Drupella* at Enewetak, Marshall Islands', *Bulletin of Marine Science*, vol. 38, no. 1, pp. 9–11.

Brinton, E. 1962, 'The distribution of Pacific euphausiids', *Bulletin of Scripps Institute of Oceanography*, vol. 8, pp. 51–270.

Compagno, L. J. V. 1984, *Sharks of the World*, F.A.O. Fisheries Synopsis No. 125, vol. 4, part 1.

Cousteau, J. Y. 1970, *The Shark. Splendid Savage of the Sea*, Cassell, London.

Cresswell, G. R. 1991, 'The Leeuwin Current — observations and recent models', *Journal of the Royal Society of Western Australia*, vol. 74, pp. 1–4.

Cropp, B. 1975, 'Riding the whale shark', in *Sharks and Shipwrecks*, ed. H. Edwards, pp. 69–75.

Davenport, S. & Stevens, J. 1988, 'Age and growth of two commercially important sharks (*Carcharinus tilstoni* and *Carcharinus sorrah*) from northern Australia', *Australian Journal of Freshwater Research*, vol. 39, pp. 417–33.

Ellis, R. 1975, *The Book of Sharks*, Grosset & Dunlap, New York.

George, J. D. & George, J. J. 1979, *Marine Life*, Rigby.

Glynn, P. W. & de Weerdt, W. H. 1991, 'Elimination of two reef-building hydrocorals following the 1982–3 El Niño warming event', *Science*, vol. 253, pp. 69–71.

Gudger, W. W. 1927, 'A second whale shark, impaled on the bow of a steamship', *New York Zoological Society Bulletin*, vol. XXX, no. 3, pp. 76–7.

Gudger, E. W. 1931, 'The fourth Florida whale shark, *Rhincodon typus*, and the American Museum model based on it', *Bulletin of the American Museum of Natural History*, vol. LXI, pp. 613–37.

Gudger, E. W. 1935, 'The whale shark at Acapulco, Mexico', *New York Zoological Society Bulletin*, vol. XXXVIII, no. 2, pp. 68–71.

Gudger, E. W. 1937, 'A whale shark speared on the bow of a steamer in the Caribbean Sea', *Copeia*, no. 1, April, p. 10.

Gudger, E. W. 1938, 'Four whale sharks rammed by steamers in the Red Sea region', *Copeia*, no. 4, December, p. 10.

Gudger, E. W. 1941, 'The food and feeding habits of the whale shark', *Journal of the Elisha Mitchell Science Society*, vol. 57, no. 1, pp. 57–72.

Gudger, E. W. 1941, 'The whale shark unafraid', *The American Naturalist*, vol. 75, pp. 550–68.

Harrison, P. J., Babcock, R. C., Bull, G. D., Oliver, J. K., Wallace, C. C. & Willis, B. L. 1984, 'Mass spawning in tropical reef corals', *Science*, vol. 223, pp. 1186–9.

Heyerdahl, T. 1950, *The Kon-Tiki Expedition*, Allen & Unwin, London.

Hutchings, P. & Saenger, P. 1987, *Ecology of Mangroves*, University of Queensland Press, Brisbane.

Jones, M. J. 1991, *Marine Organisms Transported in Ballast Water: A Review of the Australian Scientific Position*, Bulletin 11, Bureau of Rural Resources.

Karbhari, J. P. & Josecutty, C. J. 1986, 'On the largest whale shark *Rhincodon Typus* (Smith) landed alive at Cuffe Parade, Bombay', *Marine Fisheries Information Service Bulletin*, no. 66, pp. 31–5.

Kinsey, D. W. 1988, 'Coral reef system response to some natural and anthropogenic stresses', *Galaxea*, vol. 7, pp. 113–28.

Kinsey, D. W. 1991, 'The coral reef: an owner-built, high density, fully-serviced housing estate in the desert — or is it?', *Symbiosis*, vol. 10, pp. 1–22.

Macpherson, G. 1990, 'Whale shark tales', *Australian Natural History*, vol. 23, no. 7.

Marsh, H. 1987, *Development and Application of VHF and Satellite Tracking Methodology for Dugongs and Results of Aerial Surveys for Dugongs and Sea Turtles*, Report to the Great Barrier Reef Marine Park Authority.

Marsh, H. 1990, *The Distribution and Abundance of Cetaceans in the Great Barrier Reef Region with Notes on Sightings of*

Whale Sharks, Report to the Great Barrier Reef Marine Park Authority.

Mauchline, J. & Fisher, L. R. 1969, 'The biology of euphausiids', *Advanced Marine Biology*, vol. 7.

Moyer, J. T., Emerson, W. K. & Ross, M. 1982, 'Massive destruction of scleractinian corals by the muricid gastropod, *Drupella*, in Japan and the Philippines', *Nautilus*, vol. 96, no. 2, pp. 69–82.

Nolan, R. S. & Taylor, L. R. 1978, 'Mini the friendly whale shark', *Sea Frontiers*, vol. 3, pp. 169–76.

Nybakken, J. W. 1988, *Marine Biology: An Ecological Approach*, Harper & Row, New York.

O'Brien, D. P. 1988, 'Surface schooling behaviour of the coastal krill *Nyctiphanes australia* off Tasmania, Australia', *Marine Ecology Progress Service*, vol. 43, pp. 219–33.

Oliver, J. K. & Willis, B. L. 1987, 'Coral spawn slicks in the Great Barrier Reef: preliminary observations', *Marine Biology*, vol. 94, pp. 521–9.

Pearce, A. 1985, 'The Leeuwin Current as viewed from space', *FINS*, vol. 18, no. 5.

Prata, A. J. et al. 1989, *A Satellite Sea-surface Temperature Climatology of the Leeuwin Current, Western Australia*, Report to the Marine Sciences and Technology Council.

Priede, I. G. 1984, 'A basking shark tracked by satellite, together with simultaneous sensing', *Fisheries Research*, vol. 2, pp. 201–16.

Reader's Digest 1986, *Sharks: Silent Hunters of the Deep*, Reader's Digest, Sydney.

Sammarco, P. W. & Crenshaw, H. 1984, 'Plankton community dynamics of the central Great Barrier Reef lagoon: analysis of the data from Ikeda et al.', *Marine Biology*, vol. 82, pp. 167–80.

Silas, E. G. 1986, 'The whale shark (*Rhincodon typus* Smith) in Indian coastal waters: is the species endangered or vulnerable?', *Marine Fisheries Information Service T. & E. Series*, vol. 66, pp. 1–17.

Simpson, C. J. 1985, *Mass Spawning of Scleractinian Corals in the Dampier Archipelago and the Implications for Management of Coral Reefs in W.A.*, Bulletin 244, Western Australian Department of Conservation and Environment, Perth.

Simpson, C. J. 1991, 'Mass spawning of corals on Western Australian reefs and comparisons with the Great Barrier Reef', *Journal of the Royal Society of Western Australia*, vol. 74, pp. 85–91.

Smith, H. M. 1925, 'A whale shark (*Rhineodon*) in the Gulf of Siam', *Science*, vol. 62, p. 438.

Stevens, J. D. (ed.) 1987, *Sharks*, Weldon Owen, Sydney.

Taylor, J. G. 1989, 'Whale sharks of Ningaloo Reef, Western Australia: a preliminary study', *Western Australian Naturalist*, vol. 18, no. 1, pp. 7–12.

Taylor, J. G. 1990, *Whale Sharks of Ningaloo Reef*, Report for Australian National Parks and Wildlife Service.

Taylor, J. G. 1991, *Whale Sharks of Ningaloo Reef*, Report for Australian National Parks and Wildlife Service.

Turner, S. 1992, Drupella cornus: *A Synopsis*, Department of Conservation and Land Management Occasional Paper No. 3/92, Western Australia.

Wiebe, W. J., Johannes, R. E. & Webb, K. L. 1975, 'Nitrogen fixation in a coral reef community', *Science*, vol. 188, pp. 257–9.

Wilkinson, C. R. 1992, 'Coral reefs of the world are facing widespread devastation: can we prevent this through sustainable management practices?', *Proceedings of the 7th International Coral Reef Symposium*, pp. 11–21.

Wilkinson, C. R., Chou, L. M., Gomez, E., Ridzwan, A. R., Soekarno, S. & Sudara, S. 1993, 'Status of coral reefs in Southeast Asia: threats and responses', in *Global Aspects of Coral Reefs*, ed. Ginsberg, University of Miami Press, Miami.

Williams, D. McB., Wolanski, E. & Andrews, J. C. 1984, 'Transport mechanisms and the potential movement of planktonic larvae in the central region of the Great Barrier Reef', *Coral Reefs*, vol. 3, pp. 229–36.

Wolfson, F. H. 1983, 'Records of seven juveniles of the whale shark, *Rhineodon typus*', *Journal of Fish Biology*, vol. 22, pp. 647–55.

Wolfson, F. H. 1986, 'Occurrences of the whale shark, *Rhincodon typus* Smith', *Proceedings of the 2nd International Conference on Indo–Pacific Fishes*, pp. 208–26.

Wolfson, F. H. & Notarbartolo di Sciara, G. 1981, 'The whale shark, *Rhiniodon typus* Smith, 1928: an annotated bibliography', *Atti. Soc. Nat. Museo Milano*, vol. 122, nos 3–4, pp. 171–203.

PICTURE CREDITS

All photographs are by Geoff Taylor (© Geoff Taylor), except those listed below, which were supplied and reproduced with the permission of the following organisations:

page 39, Mansell Collection, London; page 42, Neg. No. 312923, courtesy Department of Library Services, American Museum of Natural History; page 43, Neg. No. 292265, courtesy Department of Library Services, American Museum of Natural History; page 50, reproduced with permission of the Executive Director, Department of Conservation and Land Management, 50 Hayman Road, Como WA 6152, and acknowledging the contribution from the Remote Sensing Application Centre, Department of Land Administration, Midland Square, Midland WA 6056; page 133, courtesy Alan Pearce, WASTAC, CSIRO, Western Australia.

All illustrations © Angus&Robertson.

PERMISSIONS

The quote on page 4 is from *The Poetry of Robert Frost*, edited by Edward Connery Lathem. Copyright 1944 by Robert Frost. Copyright 1916, (c) 1969 by Henry Holt and Company, Inc. Reprinted by permission of Henry Holt and Company, Inc.

The publisher would like to thank Thor Heyerdahl for permission to reproduce the quote on page 46, which is from *The Kon-Tiki Expedition*, 1950, HarperCollins Publishers Limited.

INDEX